A Woman Remembers
(everything)

Praise for *A Woman Remembers (everything)*

This powerful book is deeply insightful to the very real and heart-breaking experience of narcissistic abuse. The author provides inspiring hope to the reader through an awakening of strength and healing from the emotional and physical scars and creating the life she deserved all along. —MS

A Woman Remembers (everything) is a riveting piece. The book is a journey through life challenges over a span of years as a wife, mother, friend, and as an academic. J. Byrd has a depth of knowledge of the human condition that helps her navigate the many complexities in this world—some with life-or-death consequences. Her awareness of people and all of those around her is remarkable. Much of this life transition, depicted by the author, was far from ideal—but she chose to carry on for the good of her children and self—navigating a minefield of questioning family and friends and jumping off the proverbial cliff toward a new life. This book takes you through her kaleidoscope of experiences and emotions—"shaking you" so you can follow her through the process together. —PC

A compelling memoir, "*A Woman Remembers (everything)*" tells the story of a smart, fierce, strong, and resilient woman. A survivor of domestic abuse, J. Byrd ultimately moves cross-country with her four children to accept a position as a professor on the East Coast. She faces multiple challenges, juggling life as a single mother and highly accomplished teacher and international lecturer with wisdom, courage, and remarkable self-awareness. Despite criticism from "friends" and family regarding her choices, she stands firm and begins a new life with her children. Though waves of realizations about how the trauma from her former life continue to surface and cause periodic self-doubt, her courage prevails through medical challenges, the loss of a parent, and a global pandemic. Her writing is at once eloquent, funny, wise, inspiring, and at times horrifying, yet always she returns to hope, and gratitude for new beginnings.—NY

A Woman Remembers

(everything)

J.BYRD

THE BLACK CROW

WESTERLY, RHODE ISLAND, UNITED STATES

The Black Crow Publishing

Westerly, Rhode Island, United States

Copyright ©2025 by J.Byrd. All rights reserved.

Library of Congress Control Number: 2025903150

Paperback ISBN: 979-8-9913693-0-5

eBook ISBN: 979-8-9913693-1-2

Book cover and interior design by Christina Thiele

Editorial production by KN Literary Arts

theblackcrowpublishing.net

theblackcrowpublishing@gmail.com

For my girls, may they always stay true to Ophelia.

For the love of my life, Charles, who saw me and continues to see me even when I do not always want to see myself. Thank you.

For my father and mother, who supported their expressive and "out-there" daughter. I love you, and I miss you both dearly.

And for my dear friends, who loved me even when I was unlovable.
CDKRG

Oh, and thanks R.B.

j.

Content Guidance: Some of the text includes violent imagery, sexual assault, rape, abandonment, conversations regarding death and dying and strong language.

Note: No legal or medical advice is being given by the author in this book.

Table of Contents

I am

Holding in my hand
A Crystal
Multifaceted
Fractured Light
Reflection of Life
Representative View
Perspectives
Me

j.

Prologue

This story is not about him—thank God. Rather, this story is about a woman transformed or, more accurately, rediscovered, despite it all and perhaps a little bit in spite of him. Now I realize that it is a one-sided story. I am not writing an objective recall of events for research publication—how absolutely freeing that feels. I am sure that "the form of a man" would have his view and that it would differ greatly from my own, but I really don't care, and I make no sincere apology. This book is sprinkled with notes, writings, etc. that were created over a period of nearly twenty years. So, with all that said, I know what I lived and experienced—from the moments curled in to a ball of sobbing tears to the moments of victory and euphoria found in my new freedom—and I would like to share it with you.

The book is divided into three parts, or acts: A Woman Paused, A Woman at Play, and A Woman Undone. Each act reveals the process of becoming, providing a glimpse into the transformation, and takes place at different moments in time spanning over many years.

I am taking you by your shoulders.
And.
I need to shake you (a bit).
Follow me.
We are going to get through this together.
j.

Breathe.

A Woman Paused

———————

Just the Facts

I was nearing the end of my PhD program. I had completed all my coursework and comprehensive exams and had defended my dissertation proposal successfully. I was one project away from earning my doctorate and was approaching the process of seeking a teaching position at another university. This milestone—the completion of my doctoral studies and the beginning of my professional career—would not only be a significant accomplishment but would also be an investment in our future and our children's future. My success was vital for reaching our family's goals—and my own.

By this time in our lives together, my husband and I had been married for twenty years. We had four children, a dog, a cat, and multiple other small furry creatures inhabiting our idyllic suburban home in the Midwest. Our children were successful in school—attending solid academic programs, traveling abroad, and participating in several extracurricular activities. We had an interesting assortment of couple friends with whom we spent much of our free time—hosting dinners, traveling, and celebrating holidays.

From the outside looking in, our professional lives, our home, our children, and our friends appeared to be picture-perfect. In many ways our lives defined success—I suppose I "had it all."

However, my life was building up to a natural point of change. Over the years we had worked toward achieving individual and common goals—earning degrees, preparing children for college, investing in our home and belongings. When the timing was right, and we had taken all the steps to reach the summit of our dreams, we would take the next grand gesture—whatever that would be. We had anticipated several changes in our lives: new jobs, moving and buying a new home, and the emptying of our nest. Finding ourselves on the top, peering over the edge, it was clear that the time was here. I could see the next steps—or leap—that we'd need to make. This leap would change our lives forever, but this is what we had talked about, agreed upon, and worked toward—it was why we had sacrificed all our time, sweat, tears, and late nights.

I was ready.

I was ready for several reasons and sought this movement in our lives. I embraced the idea of change and looked forward to this transition.

I was ready to take my place in academia.

I was ready.

He was ready.

He thought he was.

I thought he was.

So, we made the decision to move forward. We would make a significant life change and had prepared ourselves—as much as one can for an approaching life transition—for a new Midwest or Coastal lifestyle.

But what others could not see, and what I would not allow myself to acknowledge, was that our willingness to move forward and in the same direction was not in balance. Privately, my husband was hesitating and redirecting. Although his actions appeared to be in unison with mine and he seemed supportive on the outside, his mind, heart, and soul were not. At the time of change, two paths appeared, and we chose different directions. The result was the slow and painful demise of our relationship. Our "picture-perfect" marriage was fading—leaving only the empty reality to remain.

How does one act and move into and through the abyss?
j.

At every point of change there comes a time when one must decide to fall forward, releasing past assumptions to begin again and ending clarity to enter the soupy mixture of transition.
I let go.
j.

Sometimes it only takes a spark to ignite a rapid rhythm of change, and on one afternoon, in the heat of the day, his actions catalyzed my reaction. He was a pathological liar. I never knew where we were in terms of our relationship, finances, etc. If I pressed him or cornered him in a lie, he would become violent. On this day, he was upset about one thing or another, a circumstance of little matter, and he entered the room in a fit of rage. His temperament was like that—dull, vacant, and absent in one moment and then full, vibrant, and explosive in the next. Basically, he was a ticking time bomb, always waiting for me to set him off. This was the last beating I took before I said goodbye.

It Begins with an Ending

The floor.

Tile.

Blue, gold, mosaic vinyl and smears of glue.

The base of the toilet.

A R C H

The ceiling.

B E N D I N G   U P W A R D

The tile floor.

A R C H

Black. . . .

. . .

. . .

. . .

. . .

. . .

Sparkles of light.

Dancing behind my eyes.

His face.

Angry.

Swollen.

Red.

Grimace.

Angry.

Red.

Swollen.

Grimace.

Black. . . .

. . .

. . .

. . .

. . .

My ears ringing.
Buzzing.
Hmmmmmmmmmmmmmmmmmmmmmmmmmmmmmmmmm.
Buzz.
I could feel his grip.
His fingers.
Interlaced.
Around my throat.
Tightening.
Pinching.
Compression and force.
Tightening.
Tightening.
Tightening.
Tightening.
His mouth—moving.
No words heard.
His lips pursed, then parting.
Teeth gritting.
All done in silence.
My ears ringing.

Ringing. Ringing. Ringing. Ringing. Ringing. Ringing. Ringing.
My eyes lift to the doorway and there . . . she stands.
Her face in shock and disbelief.
Looks upon her father hunched over my bent and contorted body.
Strewn backward over the seat.
His knee pressed against my breastbone.
Hands wrapped around my neck.

She gasps.

9

My eyes flit between hers and his.
Fear sets in.
I feel fear—for the first time—real fear.
Not for me, but for her.
Standing there in the door.
Would he go toward her?
I g - l - a - r - e at her to leave.
He catches my silent actions and turns to see her face—
she was disgusted with him.
He pauses.
His grip loosens but remains, deliberately resting and waiting.
His knee, though, digs deeper downward into me—and, with a final
thrust, a spiteful one at that, he whips his face back to mine.
"You fucking bitch, I hate you—I fucking hate you—I want you dead
you fucking bitch!"
One last squeeze—for good measure.
One last thrust of his knee—to let me know that he is there and then—

RELEASE.

I lie numb.
Arched backward over the toilet—motionless.

My body floating above me . . . I cannot hear. I cannot cry.
Pain has yet to find me.
Numb.
The door creaks open, and it is her.
I find some energy to stand and stumble only to push her into the hall.
"Hide in your room and lock the door—all of you. Go to sleep."
A door slams downstairs and a car speeds away.
I slowly close my bedroom door.
Defeated, I crawl on top of the bed.

Between the covers now I feel the bruises rise to the surface.
I can't swallow.
I fall into sleep.
Sleep—a deep sleep.
Now I realize that I have been sleeping—for years.
Sleepwalking in this horrible life, and today it could have truly ended.
I could have ended.
I hate the floor.
I hate the blue and gold vinyl.
I hate it.

j.

When thinking back to this part of my life, it seems like decades ago or perhaps even a story of another's life, not my own. I can hardly retrieve the ordinary details of life back then. The little things like my house number, the color of my couch, or the names and faces of my neighbors—gone. You would think that the particulars, the everyday stuff, would be easily remembered. Lord knows the number of times I polished the furniture, dug in the garden, walked the sidewalks, and visited neighbors. But these images, like the pains of childbirth, time has blocked out while I shed one life to forge another. Despite my apparent amnesia, I do, however, remember vividly the emotions and feelings I experienced in that lifetime. This was not the first, second, third, or fourth time that he abused me—financially, mentally, but mostly physically. He had this obsession with wanting to take the breath away from me through either choking or covering my mouth and nose with his hand. He thought it was funny and would often laugh during or afterward and tell me I was overreacting. This was his power over me. At over 225 pounds and six feet tall, he had the strength and the ability to overwhelm my small frame. But his favorite method, as I just described, was to both choke and place his knees into my chest, compressing my lungs. I could not breathe. This was usually followed by him raping me. It was brutal, and I felt like an object. Times before, he would threaten me and would pull me down the staircase by my hair. At times he would take it a step further by either attacking our dog or by yelling abusively at the children after he finished with me. I would often go to my friend's house with the children and pets to hide from him. I reached out to support services, but I could not go. I was afraid. He was dangerous—he still is.

I never felt like I belonged *there*—in the Midwest. Never. Not even as a small child, as I distinctly recall conjuring make-believe stories in my head that I was accidently born to the wrong set of parents and that my life would be spent seeking "home." Living in the heartland, I felt trapped, landlocked, chained to the conformity of traditional roles—I was swallowed by the vast prairie, drowning in a beige sea of grain. And perhaps that is why I left the first time in my early twenties—to escape to adventure and possibility. Unfortunately, my liberation was misguided and drove me toward a doomed union, which stirred these ingredients together into a gooey batter that would fester and rise into a marriage. I was thinking at that moment of my youth that I just wanted out, to get away, and who better to do that with than my childhood friend? It made rational sense at the time: Marry your friend. Isn't that what marriages should be based on—a core of friendship? He was from what appeared to be a good family that owned a successful company, providing me with a sense of financial security and stability. He seemed to be a "good catch." Soon after our wedding, we moved from one coast to the other, but much of our time was spent apart. He was serving in the military and traveling, and I was journeying within, spiritually and academically. The beginning of the end came with his declaration that we would be moving back to the center of the earth—the Midwest—so he could work for the family business. I returned with him, reluctant and scraping my nails across the miles of pavement. To compensate, I filled my life with things and thoughts. If I could not physically be somewhere else, I would create a nest that would transform the space. I found myself immersed in the university both to create distraction and to stimulate my life with wonder and conversations of both the practical and theoretical. It was there that I would hide for years. At the time I did not recognize that I was sheltering myself from my life, but looking back, I can see it now. The library stacks became my place of solace and the classroom my refuge.

One can only go on living two lives for so long before the two splinter at the point of transition. As I neared graduation and faced the imminent loss of my sanctuary, the hollow state of our marriage was revealed. Our relationship had crumbled, and our identities were so diverse I could no longer relate or interact with him in any meaningful manner. I was no longer the young bride romanced by potential; I was a woman, seasoned by experience, childbirth, and higher education, and driven to explore beyond the boundaries. I cannot fully explain the feeling I had inside me, that emotional longing so intense to move forward—toward a life with meaning. I tried to suffocate my emotions and just be who I had become. I was miserable.

So, I jumped.

> *"She drove out of here like a bat out of hell!"*
> *—Quote from a friend*

It is funny what memories stick in your brain. Generally, it is those important milestones that do—the moment when he asked for your hand in marriage or the first time you saw your child's face. I remember the beautiful hot August day of my liberation. I have the image of the Interstate 80 exit and my minivan's dashboard seared into my memory. I drove hard to my new life, barely taking a moment to pull over to sleep and eat. It felt like I could not run fast enough, and if it were not for the Atlantic Ocean, I might have kept on going.

After miles of highway lay in my rearview mirror, I ended up in a parking lot late at night with a set of apartment keys, a couple of friends, and a sleeping baby. I did not realize what I lacked, in terms of stuff, until I completely unpacked and found myself swimming in the empty, stark-white and beige apartment. I was without a stick of furniture, but I had books, a laptop, toys, a few random pots and pans, toothbrushes, and assorted clothing. I guess those are the basics of what one needs to restart a life. I was about to experience the joys of living in an "empty zen state."

———

This was not how it was supposed to have happened. The move was to be a mini end-of-summer vacation to the East Coast. We would pull a trailer of the things we would need to live in the university town. The children would get to visit the ocean—they were excited and had their bags packed and ready next to the front door. We waited for him to arrive with the trailer. He did not come. Then, later at night, he drove up the drive, burst through the door, and said, "I am not driving you. I will not help you leave." The girls broke down in tears. He yelled at them to move their suitcases back to their rooms and unpack. This was not a viable option for me. I had to go—professionally there was no other alternative. I ran to my van and began tearing out the extra seats and throwing all the boxes and bags that I could inside. I called my friends and family to come and help. My girlfriends handed me gas cards. My soon-to-be-ex was found working on something under the hood of my van. He said he was checking oil levels. It was shortly after, we were off. When we arrived at our destination, the van's serpentine belt fell off. The engine and belts were covered in oil. Accident? Coincidence? By grace we somehow did not crash on the interstate. "Jesus, Take the Wheel" by Carrie Underwood became one of my favorite songs.

Distance is a friend. It brings clarity and focus to what might have been obscure while in our intimate embrace.

j.

In my other life, I was too busy to notice him. I was working two, three, and sometimes four jobs and going to school full time plus taking care of kids, going to soccer games, and drinking wine with friends. Slowly, he had become a shadow in my life, lurking in the corner along with his "hidden" actions. He went from being an interactive partner to a ghost. This was a slow process, through erosion of years, and at some level I believe we both were aware this could happen as our interests diverged and our conversations rarely overlapped.

But in this empty space of a new, yet temporary, home for the next two years, I could not help but gain eyesight—both retrospective and insightful vision. With little to nothing to distract my attention, I found I had a lot of free quiet time with myself— my mind, my thoughts. My apartment became a looking glass and amplifier to my inner voice. I created a nest that was kind, soft, and comforting—it even smelled nice. I enjoyed the peace of my new home; there were no discussions or arguments over the petty day-to-day issues buzzing through the halls. No picking up after an "adult" child or dealing with his lumbering presence molded to the couch, mesmerized by the flickering images on TV while eating a bag of Cheetos. No, in my new space I found joy in the simplest of moments. If I wanted to eat scrambled farm-fresh eggs with local blueberries for dinner with a glass of pinot grigio while watching *Under the Tuscan Sun* for the fiftieth time or have dreamy and creamy Thai massaman curry chicken take-out three days in a row, then so be it. I was free from "What's wife cooking for dinner tonight?" and from the labored discussion over which fast-food or big-box cookie-cutter chain buffet value restaurant we would visit next. In my new life, food—simple food—became a passion and a delight.

In my new aloneness I also discovered that I embraced my personal level of accountability. Sure, I had moments of fear when I realized that I was my own safety net, but I knew that if I completed something, I could take the glory, and the finger could point only one way—toward me—and that was comforting.

I remember the exact moment when I could see him in clear view within my life. This clarity, oddly enough, was from a thousand-plus miles away. The acute vision came in the form of a phone call, confirmation of all my suspicions. It was one of my girlfriends. Her voice was tentative, like a doctor's before sharing a serious diagnosis. Without too many niceties she blurted out, "Your husband is having an affair and is about to leave you!" She had learned of this from a close friend of ours who bumped into him at a bar while he was on a date with another woman. There was a moment of silence, perhaps two. And then it sunk in. "Huh. Wow. That did not take long," I droned. If my memory is correct, I had only been away for about a week at this point. He must have been lonely—note the smirk here. But the time apart had little to do with the revelation, as I am quite certain this was not his first "friendship." My absence had been like turning on the lights—it had eliminated the dark corners where he had been dwelling. Not to completely compare my ex-husband to the scurrying of a cockroach along the edges of the kitchen floor, but, as they say, if the shoe fits . . .

The reactions to his indiscretions varied wildly from disbelief to rage, and from confirmation to amazement. Interestingly, some of the people I considered to be my extended family and friends were quick to blame me for his actions. According to some, if I had not left to take this academic placement, moving across the country, then he would not have had the need to fill his time wrapped around some other woman's body. I remember being so angry—no, pissed off—at the chorus of voices suggesting my neglect and limited availability to him as a wife to be the catalyst. And yet at some level I agreed to carry some blame—a microscopic smidge. But before

I fully accepted culpability for the destruction of the relationship, I asked my soon-to-be nonfriends and nearly excommunicated family a few simple questions: So, are you saying that my working to support our family and home was inappropriate and therefore the poor, neglected son-of-a-bitch had the right to blow thousands of dollars on who-knew-what and have random affairs with women?

Really?

Thoughts on Absurdity: A Conversation and Just a Bit of Salt and Vinegar

"You've got to be kidding . . . right? I mean, that does not sound like the guy I know," they would say.

There was a lot that they did not know about him—that knowledge we keep quiet within our sacred little boxes.

"He could not have possibly done that. Are you sure you have *all* the information? Because you *are* over 1,200 miles away," they would question.

The story was, I admit, a bit bizarre. Regardless, it hurt that they were questioning my story—my integrity. These were my close and dearest friends. Why would they think I would lie about something so painful?

"No, really, it is true," I would say.

To give them credit, they had known him for years and had never witnessed his x, y, and z behaviors. Or, if they had, it was only a glimpse, quickly dismissed or covered up by me. I was a perfect partner for his indiscretion. He was a soccer dad and had worked with their children for years. As a result of his involvement, he had built up their sense of trust.

Embarrassed of my situation, I felt myself shrink inside. How silly of me to share. Here I was completely revealing my personal relationship, the freakish soap opera that had become my life. No wonder no one talks about their pain, shares their true sorrow, or reveals abuse in their lives—because you find yourself on the stand, defending your life or the choices you have made. Thinking back, I did hide my pain deep within, and now, the "reveal" appeared to be out of place and absurd. This was my fault for wanting to wish it away—the suppressing of a reality to fit into a "plastic" life (one in which you mold into what is expected—to fit in, to receive accolades, and to "succeed").

Now, after shattering that life (the relationship, the identities), when I attempt to remember him, the luster and shell of the man I once knew as husband, friend, and father of my children seems to crack and shed off of his body. What is left is this mass, a form, lying beneath the surface. Not the boy I had met at twelve and fell in "love" with at the swimming pool. Not the man I had eloped with, had children with, and had dreamed a life with—twenty years vested in each other, in a life together. I had never fully seen this flesh standing in front of me before. No, this man—no, not a man, this amorphous creature—was and still is unknown to me.

Putting away the venom of this relationship, what is left is this strange sense of absurdity—an absurdity about the relationship but even more so about the onlookers, family, and society in general.

Why do people passively watch as women (or men) are left abandoned with children in tow to make ends meet, while the absent one runs and hides, free of contributing, free of providing comfort, free of sharing the responsibility?

(I don't get it, and yet I have been guilty of doing it as well. I have been told countless stories of acquaintances whose spouses left them to create new lives for themselves with little or no regard for the others under their care—causalities of escaping, I suppose. And although these stories made my stomach wrench, I did nothing or at least nothing of great measure to aid. Looking back at my lack of action, I am appalled at my own behavior.)

The absurdity goes beyond the actions or lack of action by one or both partners in the separation or divorce process. It lies in the acceptance of such behavior by others. Often it appears as if society (people in general, friends and family in particular) stands there shrugging its shoulders—easy, divorce them, and with a carefree flip of the hair, it is just accepted. Just deal with it and move on—right? I found myself over the year whispering under my breath, "Shame, shame on all of you." Hell, sometimes I would even dare to say it out loud.

The most hurtful and cutting absurdity came from other women, outsiders to the process who enabled the shameful behavior to continue. Other mothers, especially grandmothers (using that word very loosely here), who would watch children cry and yearn for their father, a father who refused to respond by phone call, email, or letter—these women would simply turn away. The best line ever, in relation to this absurdity, came from a grandmother in response to a plea I made to connect her son to his children. Her line was, "He cannot talk to them right now; he is having a hard time." She said this without a waver in her voice.

Stunned—absolutely stunned—into silence, I could not respond. Then my thoughts turned to the piles of unpaid bills, the empty refrigerator, the car running on fumes, and how I had to keep telling the kids no, no, no with each request for new clothes, high-school pictures, or money for the movies. I thought to myself, *He is having a hard time? That piece of shit.* In some strange way, I felt violated by this woman for protecting this "man" in this manner and placed shame on her for such a lousy response.

Shame on her. Bitch.

But in his silence, I emerged. For that, his absence and silence, I thank him. Because of his lack of action and lack of voice, I have been able to become and simply be . . . me.

Thank you, form of a man. Thank you.

He had abandoned the children and me. As I moved them across the country to join me, he simply slipped away. He refused to speak to the girls and would not call them on special days like their birthdays. Their hearts were broken. As weeks and holidays passed with his absence, all our hearts hardened. And maybe that is what was needed so I could break away to discover our new lives. When things cease to operate properly, says William Bridges, author of *Managing Life's Transitions*, there is a defining moment. You can embrace the moment as a signal that it is time to let go (recognizing the ending) and enter the neutral zone (transitional phase), or you can choose to ignore the indicators and settle to repeat the broken pattern. I stood in the doorway, juggling options, and with a big breath crossed the threshold.

I was free from him now. However, I was in a state of upheaval. During this time, I would cry—most heavily while in the shower, away from my children, to both protect them and preserve my privacy and pride. I showered a lot. My friends, those who undestood the situation fully, would take my late-night calls and countless emails to help carry me through this time. To let them know where I was in this process of change, I started to write them letters and prose. These were often accompanied by a photo—as to share that not only was my inner world changing, but also my appearance. Many of the selections you are reading come from letters that I wrote to my friends back then—now my past life.

In some respect, I felt as if life was on pause—I was a woman paused.

Thoughts on Being Paused

Part of my reluctance to walk through the doorway in my life comes from knowing the door will close behind me. And as I pause at the door, I realize that there are parts of my life I have cherished so deeply that moving my foot from that threshold is more difficult than I had ever imagined. What I have come to discover, in this reflection, is that many of the cherished aspects in my life are both real and imaginary.

But it is more interesting to talk of dragons and castles first—the imaginary tales of an imaginary marriage, soulmate, and kingdom. I wanted so much to believe in the illusion. Admitting to myself and embracing the knowledge that the life I had led for twenty years has been false is a difficult task. Walking through the doorway confirms the fantasy is just a fantasy, and the life, identity, and relationships within are over. I have never been good at endings—so I pause.

The cherished parts of my life that are real are what have been lodging my foot against the door for fear of losing them—my family relationships, my circle of friends, and the alliances of women. Being removed, for what appears to be much longer than a year, from this web of women, whom I adore, is extremely saddening. With each milestone, holiday, event, and birthday, I long for the sense of belonging, trust, and companionship that our group has provided over the years.

Isolation, even when self-prescribed, is a harsh medicine.

As my foot creeps along the edge, slipping closer to the brink, I feel its weight, and I am tempted to step back in to relieve the pressure, to return to what I know and where I find comfort.

"Maybe it can be fixed?"
"Maybe I caused all of this?"
"Maybe I am to blame?"
"Maybe if I would have . . ."
"Maybe if . . ."
"Maybe . . ."

But my heart knows this is not true, and I am hanging on to a life that has already passed. The woman I thought I was is gone. The one that stands at the threshold is the one who remains. I breathe in . . . a deep sigh of a breath and hold it.

My fingers run across the door, lovingly feeling the panels, the ripples in the wood grain, the numerous paint chips, and I pause . . . holding for a moment to say: "Thank you for carrying me to this point in my life with your support and love. This has been a difficult year, and I realize I have tapped each of you with my pain and sorrow. I am ready to let go of the door now—so I may heal and grow into the next half of my life—so a new woman may emerge who is wiser, stronger, and daring to live. I realize now that I do not have to lose all of you to let it go."

The door closes.

Lead, Follow, or Get the Hell Out of My Way: Dare to Live the Life Uncommon and Create a Poetic Life (A Letter to My Friends)

Dear Friends,

Is it late at night or is it morning? Depends on how you count the hours and whether you must work the next day, I suppose. During these quiet moments between day and night when all the baby tigers are asleep, I like to sit, reflect, play, create, dream, consider, contemplate, and think of all of you—the women in my life, my circle of friends.

Tonight, my mind wandered to my recent visit—how wonderful it was to see all your faces again, hear your laughter, feel your warmth and love. You have recharged my soul—giving me the strength to move ever forward on this journey with no set destination.

I want to thank each of you once again for being there and continuing when I took a misstep and would fall on my knees in fear. You took the time from many miles away to peel me off the floor, hold my face, and tell me to keep going.

Reframe . . . Reframe . . . Reframe . . . Reframe

I realize that I have many more trips, skips, and knee-buckling falls ahead. And just like in real life they usually hit me either when I poke at it to see if it is still alive or when I least expect it—and usually from behind.

There is no time to be scared—creating a poetic life isn't for wimps.

j.

It was during a visit back to the heartland that I was able to enter our former home for the last time. I came back for medical care, potential breast cancer, with a physician who was familiar with my history, and to collect the pet left behind. I feared for him. I never wanted to go back—ever—and I was scared for my safety. Of course, when I visited the house, he was not there, and it was arranged through acquaintances that the doors be unlocked so I could enter. Technically and legally it was still my home. When I stepped inside the house, it looked oddly frozen in time. As if no one had lived on the main floor for months. The kitchen still had the remains of the food I had prepared before I left—now moldy and rotten. The house smelled of urine. I could see a perfect line of it surrounding the base of the couch and chair—too perfect for the dog to have done. Then I remembered, his best friend, another winner, told him the surest way to deter dogs from peeing in the house was peeing in the house yourself. *That dumb shit listened and followed through.* I noticed the round side table that once held flowers and photos of the children was wiped clean. As I continued to explore the home, I peered down into the basement, and at the foot of the stairs the floral arrangement and photographs lay smashed. I opened the garage to find trash and boxes of junk piled up to the ceiling and stretching across the room from the outer door to the inner—it looked like a scene from the television show "Hoarders."

I moved upstairs to find every child's room completely overturned. The baby's room was disturbing as it was smeared in feces—all over her bed, bedding, and dressers. In the master bedroom everything had been reconfigured, as if he was living in a studio apartment. A computer table, microwave, and small refrigerator had been added to the décor. It looked as if a squatter had moved in and defiled our home.

But the most alarming thing was that all the door locks to the house had been turned around. To lock someone in the house—not out. I got the hell out.

Standing

I am standing . . . amongst the rubble of my life. The storm has recently subsided and eerily calmed, but the clouds are brewing in the distance, swirling, darkening, and looming—reminding me it is not yet over. For now, however, after the sustained wake of the storm releases its grip, I am finding myself standing.

The colors in my world are swirling grey, green, and dark blue . . . the air is chilled, still, and stifling . . . however time feels absent—a vacuum, my lungs do not fill. Smothered . . . What do I do? As I look over the remains of a life lying about my feet, destroyed beyond repair, I notice that nothing, nothing, absolutely nothing has escaped the wrath of the storm. Nothing that hasn't been damaged, marred, or changed.

Although I am standing, there is a weakness in my stance; I am in shock, and my thoughts are as clouded as the approaching sky as to how to next proceed. Nothing seems sure . . . everything is a risk . . . broken glass, twisted wire, and shards of metal lie around me like a mine field . . . dreams lost, beliefs bewildered, memories tarnished, hope dismissed, and joy silenced . . .

Yet, I am standing . . .

Tattered   Empty   Fragile   Lost
Torn   Alone   Broken
Hollow   Bleeding   Bruised   Disillusioned

Yet, I am standing . . .

j.

The Zen Garden and the Air Mattress

It is funny how the mind works. When I am unhappy with a situation, I flee into a different mode of thinking—I imagine myself on a scientific expedition, a cultural study. I escape. Whether I am living in a trailer in the swamps of North Carolina, a cinderblock hotel room in Anaheim, an adobe-roofed villa in the foothills of Laguna, a cookie-cutter home in the Midwest, or an empty one-bedroom in a college town, I can survive, through reframing. Moving multiple times throughout my life, I would give up one type of lifestyle to experience another. The environment, the vegetation, the people, the culture, the food, the music, the work, the life expectations were all different from space to space. Like stage settings, my character role would evolve, and different life scripts would emerge.

There, in my temporary, transitional home on the East Coast, I lived in a zen garden with perfectly and freshly painted white walls and camel-colored carpets filling the space with their emptiness. For fun in my sacred aloneness, I would "rake" the carpet with the vacuum, creating patterns of swirls and lines. I had left a lovely Dutch Colonial with gardens, patios, and masses of trees for approximately 700 feet of empty living space. It was stark, but easy to manage. That was an advantage. And like my new life, it was an absolutely clean slate. No decorations, no dimension, no luxuries, just a calm, empty, nothing from which to conjure up my being. Well, that and an air mattress that was kindly lent to me by my research partner—a raft in the sea of carpet, its presence reminded me of what I no longer had, a bed. For months I lived this way—it was a definition of home, I guess. I read and wrote a lot and had long incoherent conversations with one of my roommates, my two-year-old daughter who spoke only a few words in broken English.

Other creature comforts included my laptop, which served as my outreach to the world beyond the blank walls, and several boxes of toys and books—lifesavers, as I converted a large walk-in closet into a magical playground for my wee one. Beyond that, nothing, and at first, I missed the belongings I once had, considering all the money and time I had spent on purchasing my booty (layers of home and holiday decorations, items for a well-equipped kitchen, books for my home library, plants for my love of gardening, and special gifts and extras for the children to enjoy) so as to display and use it. My home, garden, and life are my artistic canvases, and it takes time to curate with intention, purpose, and creativity. I realized that the markers of wealth, achievement, and tradition were gone. For a moment, a few months into the process, I felt a sense of great despair, defeat, and loss as result. But over time, these items would eventually become relics associated with life. If they were present, they might have conjured memories of a family that I had once intricately woven and tenderly nurtured. For now, they were simply artifacts of a past life. And now, without them, I was light. There was serenity and vision within the silence.

Silent

Shhhh . . . in the stillness I see more clearly.

There are times in our lives when it is very appropriate to be silent. Some of those can be brief moments, and other times the silence may carry over years . . . but in either circumstance, lying still may be the option of choice. So many times, I have covered my mouth with my hand, pursed my lips tightly, and bit my tongue to remain silent . . . why? Because there is benefit to being silent—holding presence in one's life.

Silence is the watchful eye's best friend.

To be able to see clearly it is often best to not be noticed. The wallflower sitting and watching others doing what with whom, and why, is surveying and collecting data on the social condition.

Through practiced silence the wallflower examines the world around them. Silence allows the watchful eye to focus; it quiets the mind, gives others permission to be comfortable and to act freely, and thus in turn encourages others to reveal themselves.

Silence is a partner to listening.

While one is watching, one is also listening intently. By being silent your mind and thoughts are not cluttered with your own words and utterances—you are able to quiet the inner voice. You are not "hearing" the noise while you are preparing your response . . . by not having one, you can fixate on the sound, the tone, the inflection, the meaning, the word choice. You are listening to both verbal and nonverbal cues. You hear their loud silence, for instance, when words would be most desired and appropriate. Silence and listening go hand in hand.

Silence is deliberate.

While purposely being quiet, you become more aware of your environment and, therefore, are more likely to make the appropriate choices in your next course of action. You are aware of the timing of when to make your move, speak your mind, and command the conversation. Silence is not a sign of the weak; it is thoughtful and deliberate fortitude. Silence is also the act of compassion (gentle, comforting, tender), a source of refuge (safe space, enveloped stillness), and a means of healing (fasting, recovery, loving).

Lying within the heart of the silence is both an inner strength and a depth of patience. When the silent chooses to speak or act, others are often struck by the power and force that emanates from them. Because of this, they are heard, and others listen and "see"— what was not apparent then becomes obvious.

I am studying, I am watching, I am listening, I am considering deliberate courses of action. I am lying silent.

Fortitude: That strength or firmness of mind which enables a person to

encounter danger with coolness and courage, or to bear pain or adversity
without murmuring, depression, or despondency; passive courage; and
resolute endurance. (dictionary.net/fortitude)

Navigating the Spaces In Between

Physical Space

Ending—home, the niceties
Carving a new niche
Starting over
Collecting

While walking this early period of time in the transition, I looked back at my scribbles of a working diary, and I noticed that my identities have been tied closely to various "spaces" I have occupied in my life. These spaces ranged from the concrete—my immediate surroundings—to the abstract: emotional, intellectual, and personal spaces. To make my personal transition, I found myself needing to navigate, research, reflect on, destroy, and rebuild every space— each and every space in my life—even the ones I wanted to remain untouched. I resisted, at first. It was painful.

"But this is who I am," I would repeat to myself as I cried—no, wailed—until my eyes were swollen and my nose beet-red. "How can I possibly change? What have I done? What have I destroyed?"

It was my original intent to only live in the East for one academic year, fulfilling my visiting lecturer contract as I completed my PhD. I had no long-range plans and did not come prepared to potentially spend a lifetime there. My constructed social world, fragile like papier-mâché, smashed to reveal the underlying fatal flaws in my persona—my various identities. Ones I either failed to see or refused to acknowledge.

Have I been pretending in my life? Have I not been really living a life, but acting in a scripted play of societal expectations?

The answer in the mirror was yes. (The beginning of ending.)

Shit.

Now I know that many people just suck it up and say to themselves, "Well this is what I created so I'll stick with it." But I am not that kind of gal. Nope. I cannot just let things lie, especially if they are not in order. I must straighten, and that includes the aligning of my life.

My first order of business would be to rebuild the nest and all its creature comforts.

Navigating the Spaces In Between

Cultural Space

Ending—ties, behaviors, suburban girlfriends
Discovery
Beginning
Emotional space
Ending—relationships that no longer serve, identity when in marriage, altered motherhood
Broken hearts

A Twist of Fate

Decisions.
A turn here.
A turn there.
A yes.
A no.
The acceptance.
The denial.
Each shape creates, destroys, reveals, hides, illuminates, and darkens
aspects of one's life.
We make them.
Choices.
Often without much thought.
Other times with great contemplation.
Conscious.
Unconscious.
We weave our life direction through our active selection.
Present.
Absent.
We select the colors, the patterns, the textures, the weave, and the twist.
We tug and pull.
We tie and knot.
We cut and unravel.
Until . . .
We complete and design our fate—the story of our lives.
j.

Hanging on to Ophelia

Dear Friends,

I had the strangest thing happen to me this month . . . something that I must share with you. I have met Ophelia again. I am referring to Mary Pipher's book *Reviving Ophelia* and the notion of finding the nine-year-old little girl within in each of us. The one who knows what she wants, dreams big, large and loud, and has enormous confidence in who she is . . . that little girl. The one we gave up for bikinis, boys, and dates to the prom.

I found her again.

It was twenty years since I went out on my original journey to the West Coast, when I first stumbled across her again, fell in love with her, hugged her, and nourished her. At nineteen I knew who I was once more, what I wanted and where I wanted to go in life. It was real. She, Ophelia, embodied me.

In the name of love or insanity, I reluctantly allowed her to slip away once more . . . little by little over the years, neglecting her, replacing her with what society suggested as the appropriate temperament and role that I should adopt. In her place the hollowed woman stood. Slowly, the woman could no longer withstand.

But Mercy found me, and I found her again. Escaping here, even when I felt my body could no longer withstand it, I discovered her once more. I must hang on to my Ophelia.

j.

Navigating the Spaces In Between

Relational Space

Ending—married with children to become a single, abandoned mother of four. (Gee, sounds like she would be a lot of fun to hang out with!)
Discovery.
Beginning?

A Breath of Expression

Oh, how I wanted to breathe . . . a deep and fulfilling breath . . . the sensation of it filling my lungs completely . . . open and sincere.

For years, and there were so many that I cannot recount, I had been breathing shallowly and timidly from my shoulders . . . those quick and tight gasps of air that seem to suffocate rather than provide life . . . breaths like those of a frightened rabbit hiding beneath the foliage so as not to be seen or heard. These swallows of air leave you lightheaded . . . confused in thought . . . and stifle the voice . . . small, weak, suppressed.

Over the past year, and this one I can count, I learned to breathe once again. It is like birth, entering a new world, unknown. The gasps of air at the beginning were rapid, quick, and purposeful gulps of oxygen to stay alive. I attempted to breathe in my new environment, each breath labored and painful at first, and yet feeding my body and soul. As each month unfolded, the practice of breathing slowly relaxed, the heart calmed, the shoulders released, and the lungs expanded. Over time, the practice would develop a simple rhythm, and each inhalation and exhalation would deepen toward nourishing the self.

As time continued, and of this I am fully aware, the art of breathing has become natural and complete. With each significant gentle sigh of breath is a sense of fulfillment. Every part of the body is washed in its cleansing purity. A peaceful, collected, present sense of life is created.

I am breathing a deep and fulfilling breath.
I am new.

j.

Cliff-Notes

Everyone should have someone they can stand next to
on the edge of a cliff,
toes hanging over,
body outstretched and arms held wide,
yelling at the top of their lungs, "I am alive!"
And the person next to them smiles, and totally gets it.
There is a silent and tender understanding.

All social constructs—the guards (the roles we play in life)—of our prescribed identities are shed as they do not fit, never have. Our deep friendship has transcended these social markers over the years, and as a result we are not trying to please, not trying to impress, not trying to shape, and not trying to control one another.

We just are, whatever it is we are, in whatever space, time, or "role" we are currently playing.

I am standing on the edge looking down into the abyss below.
My toes are curled over the rocks, I have just finished screaming,
and I start to laugh at my own folly.
I turn with a smile toward you and see that you are watching.
You breathe in and look toward the open sky.
It is your turn.
I am watching and smiling at you.

j.

Let Go ... Free Fall

Dear Friends,

Have you ever wondered what it would feel like to free fall out of a plane? Letting yourself go, completely, without hesitation, trusting the parachute that you so carefully folded and tucked in your sack to strap on your back. Have you ever wondered?

Sometimes we think we know why we do things or why we want them to happen or what we think we should deserve and then . . . life happens. You are in free fall, floating out of the plane, plummeting toward the ground, praying you were vigilant in checking the chute for holes, twists, or snags. There are two ways to consider this. Are you a determinist? Or a voluntarist? Do you believe that life is determined for you and that you are a puppet in the life play, or do you think you have the ability to voluntarily create the role, choose the actors, set the stage, learn the lines? There are times when I wish I were more deterministic. To give over, to allow it to unfold, to hope that it will all work out if I just let it happen. There are elements of determinism in me—especially when I say phrases like "things happen for a reason" and "there must be some divine purpose for this upheaval." Both could be considered deterministic responses.

There are times when I wish I were more voluntaristic. Leading the life I wish to lead, creating my own path and determining my own fate. There are elements of voluntarism in me as well—especially evident when I jump into a car and drive miles away (at age nineteen and again at thirty-nine) toward the unknown to recreate myself and my lifeworld.

What are you?

Both determinism and voluntarism start with the act of free fall. It is easier to stay on the plane, clinging to the open doorway—it is a sure thing. Letting go is difficult, but doable. The free fall on the other hand is terrifying, thrilling, exciting, beautiful, fearless and fearful, and both brave and stupid. It is the unknown, unscripted, and unstaged life. It is the everything-is-possible part of life.

I look down and don't see the ground—nothing but clouds. I am not reaching for the cord yet. Instead, I am spreading my arms and legs to catch the wind so I may experience flight.

Navigating the Spaces In Between

Intellectual Space

Ending
Realization that I could not think clearly at this level in this moment—
at least not in any highly critical order.
I am in survial mode.
I must let go of a dream of one path to follow another.
I have four in tow who need guidance.
Discovery and beginning are mixed together in the same bowl.

As you move into the wind you need to lean forward. Fierce and strong, and surefooted. My girls and I took a moment to practice our confident stances in our make-believe album cover shoot at the beach. The result were photos of emboldened women weathering the storm quite well. Don't we all deserve an album cover photo shoot sometime in our lives?

Four Winds

The four winds guide me and call to me. These winds navigate the course and direct me in keeping my movement steady and strong.
They are constant.

From the Wind of the West

This child of the wind brings with her the hot salty ocean air that carries with it adventure, and wildness. This wind flames the
the promise of the passions.

From the Wind of the East

This child of the wind brings with her the brisk salty ocean air that is alive and daring. This wind whispers history and old-world grace of the passions.

From the Wind of the South

This child of the wind brings with her the warm sultry ocean breezes that are gentle and loving. This wind expresses song and beauty of the passions.

From the Wind of the North

This child of the wind brings with her the wild icy wind that calls out surprises. This wind brings with it a spectrum of light expressed in an array of vivid colors of the passions.

It is because of these winds that I breathe as they infuse my body with their airs—they are my passions, my muses, and my reason for living.

Love,

j.

There Is Peace

There is something to be said about releasing a wild bird from your care when it's time for it to fly. Allowing the beautiful creature the ability to spread its wings, take flight, soar on the winds, and become what it is supposed to be within the wild.

The maintaining,
capturing,
withholding,
caging,
tending,
take up so much energy and ultimately diminish the quality of life for both the handler and the handled.
But the releasing of your grasp, to give over to the being, empowers both involved.
There is an element of joy and elation and a sustained breath of peace in reflecting on the moments that once were, that currently are, and that can now be—now that each are free.

There is serenity.
There is beauty.
There is freedom.
There is peace.
j.

It Ends with a Beginning

At some point you have to stop to start.
Stop spinning, wallowing, searching, collecting information,
asking for advice.
You just need to stop.
Breathe and listen.
I actually like being in the transitional zone—the "mean-time"—as it
is a highly creative time that is filled with possibility.
That is my trap.
I recognize it and shake its hand.
But at some point you need to decide.
Let's go.
j.

A Fortieth Birthday Card from a Friend

"Don't think of it as a divorce . . . Think of it as a 200-pound weight loss."

Thanks, friend, I am feeling lighter already.

Let Them Eat Cake

From the 52nd floor of the Pru . . .
Pinch me. This cannot be happening. I am overlooking the Boston
skyline at night . . .
City lights flickering like fireflies
Soft music and candlelight
A glass of wine
I am forty . . .
Ushering in the next half of my life on top of the world. Amazing.
And to think I could have been having cake with his family.
Let them eat cake.
j.

Breathe.

ACT II

A Woman at Play

———

April

A Tradition

May

I Have Seen Heaven

June and July

Three Dates in Paris

Exploring Little Rhody

August

Spanish Rosemary

September

Moments

October

The End Begins with a Beginning: 10/10/10

Yes, You Can Have Your Cake and the Icing Too!

The Opening: A Year, a Birthday, and a Life

I am forty. I know it is just a number and in the scope of life has no real significance. Collectively we have given this number weight, considering it to be a halfway marker between life and death—a milestone celebrated with tombstones, pokes, jabs, and over-the-hill jokes.

But as I sit here on the top floor of the Prudential Tower, the Pru, in downtown Boston, enjoying the skyline of twinkling lights, it occurs to me I am not halfway in my life span anymore. I have completed a cycle of human life, and now I am in the moment of rebirth. I have an opportunity to start life anew—and this time I have knowledge and experience from my past life to guide me and redirect me.

I decided that to keep my promise to myself—to implement this plan—I would write a monthly letter. I thought it would be appropriate to start with October, my birthday month, my night at the Pru. I closed my eyes, took a deep breath, and then exhaled my wish: a new life—one of my own design—with no limitations and no expectations (societal or otherwise) to shape me. I would be living outside of the matrix, awakened. What would it feel like from this moment on if I lived without fear or second guesses? How I would behave? What would I do or become?

I peered over the edge.
And
Pushed off.
I leapt.

Arms wide.
Eyes open and surrendering toward the surface.

It was in this frame of mind I decided at this age, I am reborn—age zero. Life before: ghosts. Still, life ahead is not void of regret or risk, but movement through these concepts in turn may lead to reward.

Regret
Regret? Maybe. The loss is great.

Risk
Risk? Absolutely. But it had to be done.

Reward
Reward? Vast opportunities can lie ahead along with freedom and self-respect.

Red Thread

There is a momentum that occurs when you find your direction.
(Note: direction does not mean "full and complete.")
Clarity? Perhaps.
You cannot wait for all the pieces to fall into place.
What you are looking for are the aha moments.
It is the gut feeling, and it is pulling you.
For me, it is my red thread. It is often best seen, unfortunately,
when you look backward on your life path—hindsight.
j.

The following selections are based mostly on one particular year in my life; however, a few come from the next calendar year. Many of the experiences are in relation to my academic career—building out my curriculum vitae with required conference presentations, etc., which were essential for me to keep my tenure track to provide for my family. You might ask yourself, "How was she able to do all of this and with children?" In my academic community, there are others in similar circumstances, and we network, watching over each other's children or even traveling with each other's families, and taking our children along to various events and conferences. My daughters quite enjoyed these travels as the settings provided them with historical and enjoyable learning opportunities. My parents would at times travel out to see me and stay with the girls as well, and as the girls got older, in their college years, the elders would watch over the littles. We were a flock.

So, I packed my suitcases and started my journey.

Suitcases—We All Carry Them

We all carry suitcases. The content of the cases changes from one person to the next, and the variation defines our characters and our life narratives. The notion that personal baggage is always negative I believe is a misconception. Even good things are packed neatly into our cases, and we carry them throughout our lives. We open the bags to review and share the content, and then we pack it all back up, preserving it for a later date. Baggage—we all carry it. My only hope and wish, for you and myself, is that by the end of our lives most of the cases are filled with adventures and interesting tales, lessons, and beauty.

Living life without regrets is one method of filling our suitcases with interesting matter. I have repeatedly said over the years that we should never say "I wish I would have or could have," but instead say yes to opportunities that come along. Saying yes requires diminishing the fear that fills your body and allowing the need, the desire, and the compulsion to thrust you forward. And although I mostly follow this mantra, there are times when the line of action seems too difficult to take. Regret quickly steps in thereafter and boldly reminds the self of what would have or could have been. I have suitcases filled with moments like these, both with and without regrets, and as a result my life has forever changed.

Creating a life narrative filled with passion, bliss, and beauty is yet another way to pack your suitcases. At my children's high school graduations my sincere wish for each of their futures was that they "live a poetic life." Oddly, I did not wish for them to get a great job, finish college, buy a house, or get married, but instead to be the authors of their lives, creating and fulfilling their passions, experiencing bliss, and witnessing beauty. I wished this for them, but also for myself. I believe in the moments when I have deliberately filled the cases with my authored lines; they have produced some of the most rewarding outcomes.

Knowing that you are carrying bags throughout your life is a powerful acknowledgement. It suggests awareness and a realization of presence. I am here now, and what I have are my experiences.

Nothing more, nothing less. I just am. With this awareness come suitcases filled with peace, harmony, and a sense of being centered. Awareness, however, can involve a glaring honesty, a candid reflection, and result in a heart-opening that fosters vulnerability. The revealing of the case contents for all to review. It is then that the self can be—just simply be.

We all carry cases, and they are ours to hold. We move them from site to site throughout our lives and pack and unpack them with our unique stories. The following are some of the contents from within my bags. Perhaps by sharing some of my narratives I will inspire you to open your cases and share yours.

October

A Year of Yes & You Got Mail

Halloween has always been one of my favorite holidays. I think it is because I love fall—the final bursts of color, vibrant and bold. Nature releases its energy in an array of hues. Fall in New England is particularly amazing—an explosion in flames of color. During this time of the year, nature defines you and your place on the planet, commanded by the sun, and resting in the universe.

It's the 31st of the month. With the girls tucked into their beds, dreaming of jack-o-lanterns and candy, I decided to log into my computer and go online.

You got mail.

And there in my inbox was a short note from a gentleman asking if I would like to work with him on a golf project for a nonprofit. I looked him up online, found his profile, and reviewed his work. At this time, I was doing a lot of side contract work with local governments and nonprofits. Note: I do not play golf and had no idea about his world, but I decided that he was my October yes. So, I replied: "Would you like to speak with me on the phone? Set up a meeting in person per chance?"

However, there was something else about him besides golf that intrigued me. Was it his smile and eyes or was it the red thread tugging at me?

You got mail.

Yes, he wrote, he would like to meet with me. However, I was leaving for Chicago in November for a girls' trip. Our meeting would need to be after my return.

November

Almost every year for the past several years my Midwest girlfriends and I would take a November trip—usually flying to Chicago for an extended weekend. Since moving away, I had not attended, but this year, for an extended celebration of my birthday, it was a gift from the girls—they bought my plane ticket and paid for my room, so I arranged for my daughters to stay with a colleague. I would be flying out of Boston to visit the Windy City.

While I was in Chicago, an email from the golf client arrived, followed by another, and another, and then finally a phone call. The project he proposed was interesting and combined not just golf, but growing the game by developing young players. It was a unique concept. He was articulate, smart, funny, and genteel. I was really looking forward to seeing him upon my return. I must admit though, I was a bit perplexed by the emotions that arose as we spoke. It felt like, even in this short period of exchanges, that there were possible additional dimensions to this relationship emerging. And no, I do not make it a habit to date clients, and now it was too early to suggest anything but a working relationship between us. It seemed, however, that we had hit it off—I enjoyed his intellect.

After I returned to Boston, our email and phone conversations continued, and beyond the project's substantive elements, I wanted to get to know more about him—the person and not just the client. As a result, I decided to take no fee for this project and suggested we move my role to that of expert advisor and new friend, and future business should be handled in the same manner, or I would suggest another consultant in my place.

I Was Looking for the Girl with Red Glasses

It was time for our first in-person meeting with one another. Our "business" was complete, and now what was left was simply to get to know each other. I only knew him from his photograph and our conversations, and the same was true for him of me. We were both very excited to explore Boston together. I told him he could find me in the train station bookstore and that I would be wearing my red glasses, the same ones from my profile picture. I would be traveling on commuter rail and he on Amtrak. Leading up to this day, he—Charles—wrote a clever and flirty note to me pertaining to how our first date, dare I call it that, would proceed. It went like this:

A Chinese Menu of Options
by Charles

Proposed departure from my home for Boston at 11:10 a.m.

Option #1: Depart for home 11:40 a.m.
30-minute stay in Boston, she is displeased and tells boy to "hit the road, Jack."

Option #2: Depart for home 3:00 p.m.
3.5 hour stay, nice time, walk, lunch, handholding, tender kiss on the cheek. "Let's meet again," she says.

Option #3: Depart for home 4:40 p.m.
5.5-hour visit, nice time, long lunch, handholding, multiple kisses, lose track of time and lost in conversation. "I really like this guy," she says.

Option #4: Depart for home 9:45 pm.
10.6 hour stay, awesome time, hand holding, many, many kisses, forgot to have lunch, booked a room, and broke the bubble rule* by midafter-

noon. (*Bubble Rule: I have my bubble around me, and you have yours around you. You stay on your side of the bubble line, and I will do the same in return.)

He closed the email with: "I crack myself up!"

———————

On the day of our meeting, I went to our commuter station. I selected a time so I would arrive a little bit ahead of him. As I sat on the bench, waiting for the train, my phone rang. It was Charles.

"You are not going to believe this, but my ATM card was eaten by the machine. I have some cash, but not a lot," he said.

"No problem," I said. "Just get on the train."

After boarding my train, once again my phone rang—Charles.

"You are not going to believe this, but our train hit a deer and we will be arriving later than anticipated," he said with a rattled voice.

"No problem," I said. "Just stay on the train."

At the station I visited the bookstore. I enjoyed looking through their collection—it was calming. My phone rang for the third time. Guess who? "I just want to warn you that I am not openly affectionate. I don't want you to think that I don't like you. I am reserved," Charles said.

For the third time I responded with, "No problem, just stay on the train and find me at the station in the bookstore."

Even with my back turned to the entrance of the terminal, I could feel his presence. I turned around. "I was looking for the girl with the red glasses," he said. He was beaming. His smile—I loved his smile. He approached me and stepped into my bubble and gave me a huge kiss. I said, "Is this you reserved?" I reached out and held his hand. I know this sounds all fairy-tale/movie-like, but it was magic—our hands felt perfectly interlaced with each other. From that moment on I knew I was deeply in love with him. I knew, even if he did not, and of course he did not, I had met my husband to be.

We walked out of the station and explored the city together and from that day forward we were a couple.

Prior to meeting Charles, I had made a list of what I wanted in a life partner. I needed someone who would want to experience the world with me, become immersed in present moments—their beauty and wonder, and the slowing down of time with presence. He would see me, and I would not need to explain or apologize for being me. Life would be in congruence. Over time we had many conversations and dates, and we found that we were meeting each other's needs in partnership. What became apparent was that we were two whole people coming together—complementing each other and not two halves becoming one—and our conversations and writings to each other confirmed that for each of us. The following is a series of conversations following our Boston date, where he gave me the nickname "J.Byrd."

A Series of Conversations

Moments with You

They twist and turn, down one hallway to another room. Beyond yet another door and again, a left, a right, toward Narnia . . . looking for the wardrobe and the many little aspects of splendor . . . they search together for treasures, she leads him up the stairs, and feels him behind her . . . he reaches out and touches the back pocket of her jeans . . . she notices and smiles to herself. She loves exploring with him, be it a city, a bookstore, or a sleepy antique shop. She loves being in his space, with him in this moment. She reaches back to his hand and gives it a gentle squeeze.

My love,

J.Byrd

J.Byrd,

Right on the money! Chinese Menu Option #3 was personified to the letter on first date. One could observe in the case study analysis that the two of us "follow instructions well as they pertain to options." Call me clairvoyant, but that is exactly what we did.

I'll keep that in mind when I write the "options" for our next rendezvous! (Wink.)

It was a perfect day, perfect in every regard. I found you charming and sweet. What could be better than that. I also enjoyed the unscripted events of the day, not a better way to go.

I have a suggestion: let's do it again!

Charles

I enjoyed our conversation tonight as always, and it became clearer from this evening why I am so attracted to you. You bring out the me . . . in me. You, just being you, make me feel open and comfortable, and I can express myself. Remember I said that I am a great observer and reserve myself from others, but allow others to slowly unfold who I am, at their pace, basically, if they get me, I unfold at a much quicker pace. I reveal me.

You have done that and are doing that with me. Thank you for "seeing" me.

See you tomorrow, sweetie. I have waited a long time to meet you (years) and have come a long way to find you (miles). You are worth it.

XXOO

J.Byrd

Research Title: "Meeting the Boy in Boston"

Boy overcomes adversity in face of obstacles to reaching goals: He is able to calmly and collectively problem-solve, cross his fingers, and make the best of a given situation. Examples of this are the following: the card-eating ATM machine, the suicidal reindeer, and the late train. He is able to work through each potential block to reach his overall goal for the day, not only instrumentally, but gracefully and with humor. He does not allow these barriers to impact the overall day, but in fact, these events will now become "legend" in the "How Boy Met Girl" story.

Charles, you demonstrated a sense of adventure and embraced spontaneity. You expressed your inner emotions and sealed it with a kiss. I was knocked off my feet. And your thoughtfulness in bringing me a lovely gift upon arrival—thank you.

I am looking forward to sharing more moments with you. You have touched me.

Additional rule: Resist analysis paralysis and just be present and allow selves to fully take in the joy in finding and experiencing one another.

Many hugs and kisses,

J.Byrd

———

J.Byrd,

Two words: blown away. You swept me off my feet . . . Wow!

I thought you were awesome—pretty, smart, fun, and funny. I love your touch, your affection, the handholding and kissing.

I still smell your perfume on my shirt.

Charles

P.S. I must admit, for the record, I have a weakness. It just dawned on me that I'd like to see you and waiting until Sunday will be hard for me. Being honest should be a rule too, no? I think that it very well should be the *only* rule. As I so often say professionally when people call me from all over the US for hiring advice, I always tell them that the correct answer to finding someone (profession-ally) is that the person is a good fit. The same applies personally. Having said that, a good fit is hard to find. Perhaps we've found that in one another? Too early to tell, maybe? Let's conduct some more extensive research and find out.

———

Your emails are like chocolate—decadent chocolate. I am very picky about chocolate (as I am with men, or friends, or research part-ners—ha). I only have chocolate occasionally, so when I do it is an experience and I savor it—similarly to your notes to me. When they arrive, they are special, and I do so love reading them.

I fell asleep on a stack of papers that needed to be graded—pen still in hand. I slept with the phone next to me, so if you had an urge to call, I would be ready.

Hugs,

Your J.Byrd

———

J.Byrd,

Okay, theme songs. Ready? Colbie Caillat: "Tailor Made" and "Bubbly." When I hear these songs, I think of you.

Three things to discuss later: Pepperdine University, my father, and the perfect-fit relationship. (Thank you for this. I did not know it existed.)

Charles

———

J.Byrd,

I knew from the get-go that you are too smart for me . . . putty in your hands was not my initial objective . . . hmmm let me rethink that?

I like the whole negotiation tactic you have chosen to employ: his desires, and her desires.

(Now I made you blush.)

Charles

There are fifty-five messages sent between you and me.

I think we sorta kinda a little maybe like each other. Do you think?

XXOO

Your J.Byrd

J.Byrd,

Number 56, but who is counting.

"Eau de J.Byrd"—my shirt still smells of your perfume. What is that—lavender? Very sweet. I may not wash it until I can be close with you again.

Basking in the glow. If this is a dream, please do not wake me up.

Charles

It's cherry blossom.

Love,

J.Byrd

The administrator in me just had to jot down the rules for dating so that, if in the future or when our stars further align, or some other cosmic activity occurs, we can develop the handbook.

Rule 1: Either party may at any time regardless of time zone, upon any whim or fancy, if so moved by emotion, feel free to call the other party and if so needed leave a voice message, and if so able in a breathy voice so that the other party can retain the message for playback as long as he/she so desires.

Rule 2: Either party may at any time regardless of time zone, upon any whim or fancy, if so moved by emotion, feel free to cease and desist the interaction with other said party, however are to politely and respectfully state their intention to alter the relationship in this manner.

Rule 3: Either party may at any time regardless of time zone, upon whim or fancy, if so moved by emotion, feel free to contact the other party's list of "personal references" for additional information and perhaps a secret or two if said reference feels compelled to share. Overly enthusiastic references may be subject to additional investigation such as bribery or extortion.

Have a great day. Looking forward to talking with you on the phone.

Yours,

J.Byrd

Good morning! Another beautiful day, sunny, crisp air. Walked to my office to write, read, and organize my thoughts—including thoughts about us. Thank you for taking this next step in our relationship. I am sending you a few of my writings. Look for my voice in the work.

Yours,

J.Byrd

J.Byrd,

Wonderful stuff! You write so eloquently that I am humbled. You have a gift to connect to others that is magnificent to behold.

Okay, let's take a trip to New York. I will look at rooms and travel plans. I need to adjust my reservation. Please look at Amtrak trains. We can experience the city together. We can go in early December.

Charles

December

New York, New York

We traveled to New York City with my youngest daughter. This would be a PG-13 trip, respecting the bubble line—ha!

The city was all dressed in lights and holiday splendor. If you have never been to New York City at Christmas time, go. It was magical. I left Boston, and we joined up at his station. Together we walked the streets. Glorious. On the ride home, the train was too packed for the three of us to sit together. As the riders disembarked, spaces opened for him to join me and my daughter. What ensued was lots of holding hands, kissing, etc. What we did not know was that the conductors of the train were watching us. They thought we'd just met on the train—fast workers. When the train approached his station, he stood up, gave me a goodbye hug and kiss and started to leave the train car. The conductors seeing this were even more confused.

"Hey, where are you going?" one of them asked. Charles looked back and said, "I need to get off. This is my stop." The conductor joined with others working that day—whispering and scratching their heads. In Boston I gathered my belongings and the little one and walked off the train. At that point all the conductors stood at the front exit and yelled out, "We'd never have left you! That man was crazy." That is when I realized they had been watching and wondering all along.

When I returned home, I wrote a little something for him.

The Dance . . . Our Dance

Leading . . . a solo movement
Hindered by weights.
The expression suppressed and restrained.

Leading . . . a solo movement
Freed from the hold.
The expression is more fluid and relaxed.

Beautiful, but alone.

Following . . . a duo, movement
Patient in the embrace
The expression being discovered and learned.

Following . . . a duo, movement
Passionately it ignites.
The expression creative and illuminated

Beauty found in each other—shared—together.

January

Finding a Quiet Purpose, or, How I Celebrated This Third Month of My New Life

I had plans, here and there, to do this and that, but they just did not work out. Nor did they feel right. I kept telling myself I needed to get away, and that I needed to be alone.

So that is just what I did. I spent time alone in an environment that allowed me to just be—quiet, thoughtful, reflective. I ended up doing what I enjoy most—jumping on a train and heading to Boston to visit the inner harbor, the Commons, and spend time wandering the bookstores. Quiet pleasures I called it. In the back of my mind, I was going to Boston to "find something." I did.

Exhale

For me, solo train rides are relaxation, especially when I have no reason or specific purpose for travel. I just ride and gaze out the window. Town after town passes by and the movement and sounds lull you into a soothing state of mind. Glancing up now and then, I see others in the same frame, either locked into a book, a cell phone, or an unbreakable stare—each within themselves.

Is this what I am supposed to find?
Is there someone here that I am to meet? Have a conversation with?

When I first started this birthday year of saying yes to exploring my new life, I thought each month would bring about excitement, intrigue, adventure. I was supposed to do something, find something, and experience something—different. I redirected my eyes to the trees rushing by. I let out a sigh and began to reflect.

Huh.

I look back at a year, from where I started and where I have gone on this journey thus far—a life unscripted yet by my design. I repeat this thought to myself. A scary yet exciting place to be in a life and a bit—no, a lot—of unconventional. And it all started with an ending and a step—no, the closing of a car door.

Hmmm.

What a ride from there to here, from August to now and from one life to the next.

The momentum behind the transformation first showed itself in a letter addressed to all my friends last January—"Lead, Follow, or Get the Hell Out of My Way."

And it closed with "creating a poetic life . . . isn't for wimps." Along with the letter, a picture, one that my daughter had taken of me in my new red glasses.

That first letter had started a cascade of writings, which traced the transformation. My friends allowed me to share my point, my perspective, and voice. Each month the writing intensified.

Now, over a year later

I see.
I am awake.
I can taste life.
I am living.

On the train my mind quiets on the pleasures of the day.

The activity itself is not of importance. I just roamed from bookstore to bookstore. I would come across little venues of memories, and I would pause.

The clock progressed, and it was almost time for the return train.

"Well, that was a relaxing day, but not very eventful. And not at all what I had in mind for the month's celebration."

Bored, I walked over to the station bookstore. And there it was. What I was supposed to discover on this trip. A book, a book that I had been wanting to read for over a year and had picked up countless times at stores but felt that I was not in the right state of mind to understand or hear the message. The book: *The Secret*. I opened it on the train and completed it that evening. It was an affirmation of my transformation, the reflection of a year in my life.

How fortunate to be given an opportunity to recreate oneself—to live a second time around. And if the volume wasn't turned up all the way from spring until winter this last year, watch out . . . because I am turning it up to level 10.

Breathe

A breath in for a New Year . . . I am ready to kick ass.
Love,
j.

February

Clouds and Winding Rivers

If the last month's experience was reflecting on past growth, this month's experience is propagating new life. The seedling vibrant and new requires tenderness, protection, fertile ground, nourishment, and a gentle hand (to hold) to truly thrive. This vulnerable life requires vigilant protection and loving support at this moment of development.

Here I am—on a plane heading to a destination.

Generally, I never take a window seat. I like the aisle for the same reasons everyone states—leg room, escape route, a full arm rest. But for this flight I did not request my usual seat. It did not even occur to me to do so. As a result, I find myself pinned up against glass, looking at a runway. The engines rev, the body of the craft shakes, the people suddenly go quiet. (Ever notice others right before take-off? They are pensive. You could hear the proverbial pin drop.) The plane begins to roll forward, and per routine, I close my eyes and whisper to myself a silent prayer.

Dear God,

Please protect my children and family.
Take care of them while I am away.

Dear God,

Please keep me safe.
So I may come back to them.
Thank you, God.
For this incredible life.
For it has been filled with wonderful experiences and beautiful people.
Amen.

The plane lifts.

And at this moment of take-off, a thought occurs to me. How odd that I only seem to recite this prayer while preparing to take flight. And in those moments of prayer, a scrapbook of life fans its pages of images—wonderful images, beautiful images. And then a peaceful feeling comes over me. So strange that I do not do this— pausing, praying, meditating, focusing, visualizing, whatever you want to call it—more often. Especially as it gives me a chance to be present in my life—truly present. And by being present, even in this fleeting emergency prayer, the "better say my last words" moment, I begin to fully realize I have been given the ability to "see"—the knowledge, the presence of mind, to form introspective sight. It is a gift.

I know my purpose.
No, really, I do.
I know that answer to the question of, "Why am I here?"
I see it.
I see what I am to be and will be through You.

If I simply give over and faithfully follow the path as it guides me in my life's work and connects me so I may express and share my talents and passion with others.
I am listening to You.
I hear what life is about. The words echo.
I know.
I know that if I am brave enough to move, act, and dance with these steps, I will be fulfilling my purpose—powerful sight, the voice.

What a gift to be given and to be shared.
What a gift to be able to see—to have the lens of society lifted from my vision—and given brilliant new sight.
None of the old rules apply.
None of the constructs hold form.

FREEDOM

Open the window
Free the swift
To fly

The plane climbs and settles itself. The clouds disperse and the land is revealed. We are following the coastline. I can see the waves crash upon the shore. The land etched along the body of water appears sharp, defined. The pattern is different than the one I am accustomed to. Over the Midwest the topography is that of a patchwork quilt—it is unique and interesting how the various scraps of land are sewn together by the roadways and streams. But here, the land looks like lace. The water carves out the threads of earth into an open design. And that is when I notice the rivers winding their way to the ocean.

These are untamed rivers.

They do not flow in a straight, efficient, and effective administrative line.

They are not managed or controlled by engineers.

But why wouldn't they just cut through the landscape—powerful as they are?

But instead, rather, these wild rivers twist, turn, and appear to meander through the fields, trees, and woodlands.

In a free-flowing and nonconforming shape taking the path of least resistance.

They move forward.

My inner industrialized voice questions.

What is the benefit?

What if the river is a person moving through life?

What is the benefit in the planned, constructed, materialistic-based life to move in what appears to be a countermovement—softly, naturally, tenderly, lovingly, cooperatively?

The benefit of the straight, powerful, and swift-moving path is that it is easy to identify. The movement is measured and the motion direct and quick. It is known. However, the limitations are many. In a straight path the view is limited and as a result you arrive at the end destination early, but without sight or full experience. You race to the end with blinders on.

So what?

Who cares?

A fast race to what end?

On the other hand, the person in the life of the untamed river gently flows, breathes, sees much, and works in harmony with nature. With it and not against it, the pace and flow of the current varies, at times slow and others fast. It is natural. This path trusts and as a result, life unveils new opportunities and experiences missed by others. At the end destination, that which appears to be "untamed" has now learned and experienced much in life. It has created a complete and fulfilling one.

The plane readies to land.

The wing flaps creak into position.

The wheels thump and drop into place.

The ground now rushes beneath me, and my view diminishes.

Here.

My winding path has taken me here to a destination and, although I have been to Florida before, now it is new. Although a bit apprehensive, I am excited at the prospect of this new venture.

I find Charles's face in the crowd—I felt safe within his presence. Where he was, even if it was for a short period of time, became home for me—with each other I felt home.

March

A Phone Call to Dubai

A Group of Women
1 Trip
7 Suitcases
5 Airports
30-Plus Hours in a Food Court
40-Plus Hours in Flight
6,687 Miles—One Way
All Equals
One hell of a trip!

Not sure how to process this month's experience. What an adventure! I am still overwhelmed by the sights, sounds, and smells of Dubai—none of it yet fully processed by my mind. It is a different world. Nothing I can say and no pictures I can show will fully capture what I experienced. It was life-changing—exciting, scary, awe-inspiring—as what I experienced was the clash of two cultures existing at the same time. It felt odd; I felt lost; I could not understand the language or navigate the city. Usually when I travel abroad, I have a general knowledge as there are similarities to other areas of the Western world. Here I felt like a child learning her surroundings through scent, taste, sights, and tactile experiences.

Day One

The trip began in Boston. We changed planes in London, and then arrived in Dubai. I did not realize at the time that we were flying over Baghdad toward our destination. We were low enough that I could make out the city. Our plane was diverted to Abu Dhabi because of thick fog. We sat on the runway for two hours, refueled, then we were off to Dubai. As we neared the city, we could clearly see it from the plane, along with islands made to look like palm trees. We checked in at our hotel in the World Trade Center. As we entered our room, the telephone rang. Odd. When I picked up, it was Charles! *You have got to be kidding me,* I thought. How did he know we had just walked into the room? His timing was perfect. It was so nice to hear his voice.

We decided to head out to the streets to explore and visited Dubai Creek where we later had dinner, took a boat ride to historic sites, and visited the souks (markets). What you notice right away, as a woman, is that you are surrounded by men—lots of them, and it's very unnerving. What you realize is that you, as a woman, are not equal. Some blind tourists might think so, but they are mistaken. I had to keep reminding myself I was not in Kansas anymore, Toto. I had been coached on how to dress and behave in the city long before I arrived.

Days Two, Three, and Four

We spent the next few days at the Global Women's Conference, my reason for visiting. I had been invited to lecture during and after the conference at the Dubai University for Women. Oh, what an amazing conference site. In the backdrop was the Burj al Arab, a building fashioned after a sailboat. Speakers at the conference included Jane Fonda and Sarah Ferguson, Duchess of York. They both were wonderful and shared their respective stories. Part of our conference events included attending a desert safari and dinner late in the evening. It was wonderful. I was able to hold a falcon, receive henna painting, and be up close to camels—it was like I was a visitor in the world of Aladdin.

Days Five and Six

At this point in our trip the conference had ended, and we moved to our next venue—Dubai Women's College. We were invited to be guest lecturers and held a small group discussion with the nationals. I needed to be careful in my lectures. My research presentation was citizen participation, voice, and direct action, all topics that are bit odd to be discussing at a women's college in the Middle East.

The next day was spent at the beach, where we found some incredible seashells. Again, we took time talking to local people, sipping Turkish coffee, and enjoying the cuisine. One of my favorite memories was at a little open-air restaurant located directly across the street from a beautiful mosque. We were enjoying a dinner of hummus and an array of vegetables and bread, and large glasses of fresh watermelon juice. The call to prayer echoed throughout the city. It was beautiful.

Time To Go Home—Maybe

It was time for us to head back to the US. We approached the airport but were denied access to the building. We were bumped and ended up camping in the public food court for thirty hours. To help pass the time, and to give us some sense of comfort and protection, we spent eight of those hours in a beauty salon—receiving all the services they had to offer: pedicures, manicures, waxing, hairdos. The salon was somewhat protected. Only women could enter, and the door was shut directly behind us. In addition to receiving services, we also had access to a TV and the internet. As a result of being bumped, we had to switch airlines, fly to Germany, and then to New York. From New York we took a very late flight to Boston, and I was picked up by my colleague's friends. We arrived two days later than planned. When we got home, I simply crashed on the couch and slept for several days.

April

A Reflection on Six Months and Experiencing a Tradition

I am still recovering from my trip to the Middle East. I think to myself, *Okay, so now I am feeling a bit more like forty.* The traveling-through-time-zones and sleeping-in-airports escapades of last month are still lingering in my body—but boy was it worth it. And at this halfway point in my first year, I look back over all that I have experienced—wow! I must laugh at how amazingly different my life is this year in comparison to the last. What a difference a day makes, or in this case, what a difference a year makes. In reflecting on these past six months there is one constant: I have been able to share these moments with a very special person in my life. When I originally set off on this crazy experiment of rebuilding a life in its fortieth year, I had decided that after blowing up one life, I needed to create a new one. Either that, or I'd be letting the old life linger on, embedded in me like splinters, defined by others. But I decided I wanted to be in control. I had imagined I would be alone on this journey, but to my great surprise I found myself walking beside an incredible best friend—Charles. Beginning with my first month's trip in Chicago, he was there in spirit, sharing the experience by phone and email, to the next month acting as my tour guide to New York City, to reading *The Secret* along with me during the third month, to exploring Florida in the fourth month, and finally this past month, experiencing Dubai. He was there in a sense, with timely phone calls and frequent emails.

And that brings us to month six—April.

This month's adventure was something spectacular—again, another once-in-a-lifetime activity: going to a prestigious golf tournament. But what made this trip even more meaningful was that I was invited to experience something Charles treasured so deeply. He had been working with the event for many years, and for him this was his most prized event of each year. His invitation to experience this part of his life was an honor for me, and I felt privileged to have shared it with him.

The plane trip and van ride to the golf course, alone, constituted an adventure. I met the most interesting people. I am sure you have heard of the *Miss Manners* book and *Betty Crocker's Cookbook for Girls and Boys*. Well, believe it or not, I sat next to the illustrator of these books on the plane—a very sweet little older woman who lives in Vermont. Well, she and I hit it off, and now we plan on visiting each other. She has invited me to her little corner of the world—a lakeside town in Vermont filled with writers and artists. Does that sound cool or what? I have an original copy of the Betty Crocker cookbook from my childhood, pages stained with Crisco and chocolate-chip smudges. I had signed the inside of the book in my six-year-old handwriting, and now I am saving it for my future grandchildren.

The van ride was also very interesting. I met another older woman who made me laugh so hard I cried—not at all kidding. Sitting in the seat in front of me for three hours was this tiny little woman with an enormous bag—that she somehow got through security? The bag was filled with meat. Yes . . . dried meat from all kinds of wild animals, and I am not talking about a little salami, but one as long as my arm. Also in the bag was a very large container of jerky. And if that was not strange enough, this woman then pulled out a take-out box of sushi. Yep, you heard me—sushi. Then she asked me if I would like to see photos of her grandchildren. It is here when I lost it and laughed until I cried. From this same bag she pulled out *six* 8x10 framed photos and proceeded to hold up each one to share. The act sent the whole van into a roar of laughter. I said to her, "You have a Mary Poppins magic carpet bag!" and "How in the world did you get all of that through the airport?" She was such a character.

Finally, we arrived, and all I could think of was what a beautiful city. I love flowers and gardens, and the city was filled with blossoms—dogwoods, azaleas, camellias, and wisteria in full bloom dripping from the trees. I was very fortunate to be staying with friends who lived on a beautiful street where I would take a walk each morning, enjoying this glorious spring.

Beyond taking in the gardens, I was also asked to experience the golf event with Charles. This was such a lovely property—landscaped to perfection. I spent the day walking the course several times, and what a workout. I was able to see Tiger putt from close range. As I was walking with Charles, I turned to him and said, "You always seem to pick the most beautiful places." But beyond the beauty of the course and the excitement of the tournament, what made the trip so very special was Charles—my actual destination. I wanted to see another aspect of his life. I was able to watch him in action, and I thought to myself, *He is so talented*—a master at his trade and his ability to manage the complexity of his work. For this professor of public and nonprofit management, it was like watching perfection as a case study. And what I collected as a treasure from this trip were the new friendships made along the way. What a gift—thank you, Charles.

And if that was not enough, after flying back home, I jumped on another plane and headed for Minneapolis, where I was to attend another conference. This one was related to different aspect of my research, service learning and community action. The keynote speaker was Nobel peace prize winner Archbishop Desmond Tutu. He was the cutest and most delightful older man. What a great speaker—so human, so real, and so very honest. His message was simple: "God picks the child to deliver his message and to do his work. This next generation has much to do, and it is our duty to arm them with what they need to make a difference in our communities both locally and globally."

This month was quite a month.

May

April showers bring May flowers—and did they ever.

This month has been filled with blooms, both floral and per-sonal—with surprises in the garden and in the relationship between Charles and I.

During this month my children were also blooming in their respective interests. All just discovering, dreaming, imagining their new life in the Northeast.

"I love to paint, especially with flowers," I said as we moved a hydrangea from one spot to the next in Charles' yard. I like the whimsy of clustering the colors and planting with my children. Just like the children in our lives, our pumpkin seeds, we intertwine and bind—water, sun, earth, and sand: May these roots be deep and strong.

The blossoming of a relationship, unexpected blooms are the best of all. They add dimension to the garden, an element of beauty. What will the color be? How large will it grow? Will it come back year after year? Unknown, it is nurtured with much attention.

Protected and cared for, it thrives. Classes are over, grades are in, and graduates are on their way.

I am beginning to receive graduation announcements and photos, beautiful roses—thank you for including me in your celebrations.

So . . . "How does your garden grow?"

I Have Seen Heaven

My eyes squinting
The light shimmers on the water
Shadows play on the sand and rocks in the distance
The warmth penetrates my skin
The cool sand squishes between my toes
Breathing in the scents of surf and salt
I hold his hand
Fingers laced
Slow this moment
Capture this time
For this IS heaven on Earth
j.

June and July

Three Dates in Paris

"I'll take a room at the Mercure Paris Porte de Pantin for eight nights, please." It was difficult booking this trip—I am not sure if it was the language barrier or the process of booking. I was a bit unsure of where I was going to stay. I was going to attend a doctoral residency in Paris, and I needed to be near the conference setting. This was the first leg of my journey to France. I would be experiencing three different views of the city from three different friends who had traveled here many times before. I loaded Google Maps into my computer and studied the street view. I needed to have a head start in understanding my surroundings. I also purchased a book and CD that promised to help me learn to speak French. In the two weeks leading up to the conference, I would take time out every day to research and practice.

The flight was mostly empty. I was able to lie across a few seats and sleep my way to Paris. Upon landing I hailed a cab and asked the driver to take me to my hotel. He said, "Why are you staying there? It is not a good place for you to stay. Be careful." When we pulled up to the hotel, he once again warned me and stressed the need for me to be alert. He also said that if I needed a cab in the future to call him. He gave me his card and he drove off.

When I travel to other countries, I usually do not carry a lot of clothes. I like to purchase clothes at the site—to blend in a bit. In addition, I rarely speak. A lot can be said with a nod and some pointing. Case in point, on my street every other day was market day. Oh my, the array of colors, the beautiful fruits and vegetables, and the lovely scarves and other clothing items. I was overloaded. The first day I purchased some cherries, bread, and cheese. I was interested in several scarves for my family and friends back home. I also visited the "mall" down the street and purchased several clothing items. I went back to my room and wrote to my family and Charles. The next market day I returned to the tent with the scarves. The gentleman remembered me and began to speak to me in French. I just looked at him with a blank stare. The jig was up. I had to admit that I was a foreigner visiting the city. I responded to his comments with, "I am American." He laughed and replied in English, "But you look French, and you dress French." I smiled, bought five scarves and left the market.

My First Guide

My initial part of the trip was a week-long conference. My first guide was Dirk. He was from Germany, and we had met before at a different doctoral residency. He was interesting to follow through the city. He had his favorite bars and restaurants, and it also happened to be during the French Open—tennis. We tried to buy tickets, but to no avail. In downtown Paris, near Notre Dame, there is a city square. All those unlucky ones, like us, without tickets, sat in the square, watching the jumbo screen. It was just as fun—maybe more so, as we did not have to fight crowds.

The next day Dirk and I met for lunch. On my way to meeting up with him, I had to walk under a bridge. There were several traffic cones and taped-off areas. As I started toward the bridge, I could sense someone walking behind me. I turned. There was a young man, and he was catching up to me. Remembering what the cab driver had warned me about, I had taken to carrying my umbrella everywhere we went—rain or shine. I noticed the man getting closer. As I went under the bridge he took to running—the gap was closing. I quickly turned around, raised my umbrella, and started started spewing profanities, widened my stance, looking like a crazy-woman Loony-Toon. He stopped. I screamed a last string of profanities at him and ran to the other side of the bridge. I immediately shared my story with Dirk and other conference attendees. Others had similar stories, some not with happy endings.

Later, while enjoying lunch outdoors, we noticed a man and a woman standing on the sidewalk in front of us. As they talked and looked at maps, a man—I think it was the same man who marked me at the bridge—ran up to the woman, punched her chest, ripped off her gold necklace and then ran down the alleyway. Her husband gave chase, but to no avail. Thankfully this was one of the last nights we would stay in this part of town. Dirk walked me to my building just to be sure I wouldn't get jumped. The next day he headed back to Germany and then my second guide arrived.

My Second Guide

The second part of the trip would lead me to the heart of Paris. My dear friend, Luca, was from Romania, and he too had visited the city often. His view of Paris was that of churches, overlooks, street dining, and art. We had been friends for many years. He was one of my graduate students, and after he completed his degree, his family and mine became close.

He helped me navigate the city and move from the crime-ridden area where the residency was held to a lovely boutique hotel near Notre Dame. One of our excursions was to visit the Sacré-Coeur. Stunning. It was from here that we meandered over to the open-air eateries, found a small table outside on the steps, and people watched. Artists would come over and ask to draw a picture of us—we declined. But as soon as they heard Luca's voice, they knew he was Romanian—as were they. They pulled up chairs, ordered drinks, and joined in our evening. They wanted to hear about Romania. They missed home. After some time, we walked back out to the Sacré-Coeur to overlook the city at night. The church was all lit up in lights. Again, breathtaking.

Luca would stay for a few more days, overlapping with my next guide, Donna.

My Third Guide

My next guide was the reason I'd agreed to attend the doctoral residency in Paris. She had told me, "You never say no to Paris!" So, I talked with her husband and suggested that she join me for the last part of my stay. She only needed to buy a plane ticket and have spending money. She could stay in my hotel room. Next thing I knew, Donna was cheering on the phone. "I get to go with you!"

"*You* never say no to Paris!" I replied. The rest is history.

Donna led the way on this leg. Luca would join us. The two of them hit it off, and we had a splendid time visiting churches, gardens, little shops, and of course, the Notre Dame. The best thing about this part of the trip was that we used our umbrellas for the correct reason, and not as weapons.

On the day that we visited Notre Dame I was so excited to see the stained-glass roses. The structure was impressive from the outside. As we entered and walked down the center aisle, we could see the smaller stained-glass roses on the sides of the building. But then, as we approached the center of the church, we turned right and in front of us was the most glorious rose of all. My breath caught in my throat, and I was so overwhelmed by the beauty I started to cry. Donna said, "I thought you would have that reaction. It is beautiful, isn't it?" Words cannot fully describe the beauty of this artwork. It is the type of experience one must have in person: truly spectacular.

We had a lovely dinner at the restaurant near the cathedral. I say this because when I talk to friends who have visited Paris, they all say this was their favorite place as well. I do not remember the name, but I could find it when I return. It is on a corner, and you can see the church across the street. Here we enjoyed escargot and beef bourguignon, and several glasses of wine. We sat outside, people watching again.

On Luca's last night we visited a restaurant of which the name translates to Chicken in a Pot. It was a little, adorable, cozy establishment. The food was fantastic. I decided to order the dish the place was named for, and out came this large pot with a chicken in it. Not kidding—a whole chicken. I laughed so hard. The server also laughed as he placed the pot directly in front of me. *Silly tourist* was what was going through my mind.

The next day, Donna and I wandered the streets, taking rests now and then to pause on patios for glasses of wine. After several such pauses, we got a little tipsy. We stood on the bridge at night, viewing the Eiffel Tower lit up in twinkling lights. It was time to head back to the hotel, get some sleep, and prepare for tomorrow's train ride to Giverny—the home of Claude Monet and his amazing gardens.

The alarm went off, and we were both in pain from our wine-tour adventure of the previous day. But we needed to do this trip on this day as our time in France was running out. Somehow, we managed to get up and out the door, but it was not pretty. We walked as quickly as we could to the train station and then sprinted to the train—and just as we got on, the doors closed. It was at that point when I started looking at my photos from the previous night, while we'd been on the bridge. Let's just say my ability to take photos after drinking is not up to par. One of the shots had one of us hugging a chicken statue and another was one of us posing as a statue of a woman lying on the ground. Yeah, these will not be in the scrapbook.

We arrived at Giverny at noon. Most of the train emptied at the location with us. According to the travel guides there should have been several cars and buses to take us to the gardens. There was only one, and it was already full—we were stuck at the station. After attempting to identify other travel methods, I finally went up to the service personnel and asked them to draw on a napkin the route to Giverny. The woman produced a rudimentary map, and I went back to Donna with my plan.

Note, we were not anticipating walking several miles to see Monet's gardens. As such, we had chosen inappropriate footwear. But we were determined to see this attraction even if it meant blisters. And so, we walked. The hike took us along a walking path most of the way, through cow pastures, gardens, and people's backyards. We just kept on walking and then finally—Giverny!

It was lovely and it was worth every minute of the walk. We decided to jump on the bus ahead of the rush to take us back to the train. We were fortunate to get a seat. The train back to Paris was arriving at the station as we hopped off the bus. Although it was a whirlwind of a day, I would do it all again. And just in case I do, I kept the napkin instructions for my next trip to Giverny.

Exploring Little Rhody

It is the last day of June. What an interesting month it has been, with unexpected events.

Two of my friends came to visit me for a week of beaches, shops, and sightseeing. On the day of their arrival, we traveled to Charles's house. His little corner of the world, Rhode Island, known by the nickname Little Rhody, is postcard-beautiful and surrounded by little townships, harbors, boats, and seashores. It was great to see them, bask in the sun with them, and laugh with them. We spent afternoons on the Point just listening to the waves, watching the birds, and relaxing.

In Sickness and in Health

However, shortly after their arrival, we had a terrible scare. Charles became very ill and was taken to the hospital by ambulance. I had found him slumped over the steering wheel of his truck, unable to move, and breathing in short choppy gasps. I yelled out to my friends who were in the car to call 911. I leaned into him and told him, "I am here with you—be calm. I got you." If there had been any ounce of doubt about the commitment in our relationship and the level of admiration and love that I have for this man, or he has for me, this moment in time removed any thought of doubt. It revealed the core of us as a couple.

From his hospital bed, he reached and called for me to hold his hand and to be by his side. I gently took his hand, remained quiet, holding my breath, while the world stopped spinning. He said, "I knew you loved me, but now, I really know that you do." I added, "And I will do so for the next 140 years or more." It took several months before we would discover the number of factors that contributed to his collapse—some lung-related issues, and vertigo—all occurring at the same time.

The Wine Bottle Test

When he was released and sent back home, my girlfriends and I helped him up to his room. It was very stressful. My friends and I decided we needed to relax and have a glass or two of wine. I opened the white wine in the refrigerator, poured a glass, and took a sip. No. I did not like this at all. Then I remembered Charles had brought home a special bottle of wine to share that evening—all before the hospital situation. It was on the wine shelf next to all the other wines. One of my friends said that she was going to make oatmeal cookies, and I thought, *Hmm, I wonder how the wine would taste with those?* I attempted to open the bottle and did poorly, breaking the cork and losing half of it in the bottle. We poured three glasses and took a sip. "Wow! It tastes like velvet," I exclaimed. "This is amazing and will pair well with oatmeal cookies." All the while, Charles was upstairs resting.

The next day, he came downstairs to find the bottle semi-opened and a stack of oatmeal cookies on the kitchen counter. He approached us, asking, "How was the wine?"

"Oh, it was amazing, silky smooth. It tastes wonderful with the cookies," I replied. He broke out in laughter, but an odd kind of laughter. More like a I-can't-believe-you-did-that type of laugh. After I asked him repeatedly what I had done, he decided to call his friend, a wine sommelier, and put him on the speaker phone. "Hey, what does a 1996 Château Mouton Rothschild pair nicely with? Would it be good with, let us say, homemade oatmeal cookies?" The sommelier replied with a giggle, "Yes, and it would also be good with macaroni and cheese."

Charles continued, "So how much would this bottle cost?"

The sommelier said, "A thousand dollars."

I looked at Charles and back at my friends. Oh, what had we done?

"I am so sorry!" I nervously replied. "I had no idea. It was sitting in the wine rack alongside the twenty-dollar wines."

He started laughing, but this time it was a fun laugh. My girlfriend said, "Well, you passed the wine bottle test in your relationship."

Yes, yes, I did.

Laughter is the best medicine, and it got us through some very tense moments. But that is what life is all about. Sometimes life is so absurd or scary or fun that you must laugh. In the past several months while conducting this year-long birthday experiment, I have found my giggle again. It feels good. It feels like I am living it, not just existing in it.

August

Spanish Rosemary

I had never wanted to go to Spain. It wasn't on my bucket list. But for some reason when the opportunity for another overseas doctoral residency came about, I could not resist. We would be in Madrid for much of the residency, staying in a private college on the outskirts of the city. The first thing that struck me, once the plane landed and we boarded the bus to the university, was Spain's scent. It smelled of herbs—rosemary, in particular. Once we were at the college and I strolled the campus, I could see that the shrubs and hedges were shaped from rosemary. It was delightful as the heat from the sun encouraged the plant to release its fragrant oils.

For the first several days I focused on the residency courses. I was able to write a lot during this trip in comparison to Paris. On day two, I decided I needed to wander off campus through the gates. I wanted to explore, find a place to eat other than the cafeteria, and purchase some Spanish wines. A few other doctoral students did the same, while others stayed within the confines of the campus.

A similar thing had happened in Paris. I am not sure why people would travel miles and miles only to stare at a wall or gated fence. I came back with my bags of food and bottles of wine. I bumped into a few newfound friends, and we decided to meet up that night in front of the waterfall for drinks and treats. With pillows and blankets we met, and sprinkled in between conversations of wine and food, we discussed our research. It was here, under the stars, and with waterfall sounds, that I developed relationships with other participants from all over the world. Their research was fascinating and made mine look like old glue and wasted copy paper. The others were participating in projects in several countries, helping the poor, aiding people who had been taken in by extremists and made into child warriors. And mine—my dissertation felt like nonprofit bean-counting. I was studying adaptive capacity and sustainability and survival in times of crisis within nonprofit organizations—a lot to do with finances and less to do with service.

At this residency we traveled into the city of Madrid, shopped, went to outdoor markets, had a dinner of paella in the city square, and visited art museums and castles. The city was vibrant and colorful. We even attended a soccer match—we were in the nosebleed section, and the players looked like ants, but it was still wonderful. We also attended a dinner with flamenco dancers and a Spanish guitarist. It was amazing; I truly enjoyed this experience. One of the best excursions was a trip to Toledo (pronounced in the Spanish dialect), a medieval walled city that also included Roman aquifers. As we approached the city from afar, it looked like a mirage. Again, stunning. When we arrived, everyone spread out to explore. I went with two of my new friends. We tucked in and out of cobblestone alleyways, enjoying tapas and wine. The entire trip, from first catching the scent of rosemary to the waterfalls and stars, felt like a dream. So unexpected. I would like to go back again in the future, but also include a tour of Barcelona to visit Antoni Gaudí's spectacular and whimsical buildings.

September

I returned to school to teach another semester. After I came back from Spain, Charles and I decided that the children and I should move in with him, get a fresh new start, new schools for the kids, a new life—building upon the foundation of the last year. I was very excited to be near him as much as I could. I'd waited a long time to meet him, be with him, fall in love with him.

Moments

Moments
Inspire
Overcome mundane thoughts
Where are the keys?
Pick up the shoes.
Drive you where?

Moments
Transcend
The everyday routine and make you present
Remove you from the ritual
Lift you to the beauty
Deepen the experience of life

Moments
Breathe
They awaken senses
Open the soul

Reveal the heart
Stimulate the mind

Moments with you
Make me feel alive
Express the spiritual
And gratitude for being a woman

j.

October

The End Begins with a Beginning: 10/10/10

It is the day of our wedding. The house is finally quiet, and it is just the two of us—alone. It was his brilliant idea to have the home empty; banishing out-of-town friends and family to other assorted locations gave us a few leisurely hours to reflect and just breathe before our exchange of vows. This is the second marriage for both of us. And knowing the institution well, and having dissolved one union, one would think that entering the next would be scary and tense. But it is quite the opposite. Instead, I am finding comfort and a gentle quiet of knowing between us, as if every second of my life has been building to this day. For the first time, I feel like I am where I belong, and I'm an active participant in creating my life with him.

From our bedroom I can hear him downstairs rustling the newspaper in the kitchen and making a pot of hazelnut coffee for the two of us. I picture him sitting back in the overstuffed leather chair, dressed in his boxer shorts and still-unbuttoned, long-sleeved heavily starched white shirt, enjoying the silence. Our home has become our point of calm, and together we have created a beautiful nest with billowing gardens and comfortable interiors. Our space feels like us—relaxed. We are present and happy in being together—committed and assured—like a pair of immaculately interlaced hands, a perfect fit. Life now is simple and has been from our first meeting. I have never fully experienced effortlessness before, and it feels sheer and drapes over my shoulders elegantly.

I breathe out a long exhale and lean in over the sink to scrutinize myself in the mirror, tugging at my finely etched, descriptive lines, smudging my mascara, and diligently loosening the pinned curls of my overdone updo. I release them slightly, freeing them into romantic ringlets, reflecting the mood—then take a sip of pinot and purse my lips for a bit of Lancôme's red. I look at the woman in the mirror with a bit of wonder. She is not remotely the same person as twenty years ago, ten years ago, or even four years ago. She is like a newly birthed butterfly, one that has just emerged from her encasement, where she had lain dreaming of the day when she would finally emerge to be, just simply be who she was meant to become. The sash of beads on my gown glistens in the sunlight, and sparkles scatter across the freshly painted walls. I consider the years leading up to this instant—hurtful and so foreign to this current relationship that the memories feel out of place in this moment of joy. At points it feels as if I am living a fantasy, and I greatly fear that someone will awaken me, and I will be thrust back.

"Mom?" asks my daughter who is now standing in the doorway dressed in her bridesmaid gown. "Are you okay?"

"Yes, honey, I am fine. I just can't seem get my hair to work the way I want." I tousle it with my fingers and give it a good spray. "I hope the curls stay put. How does it look?" I turn to her.

"Beautiful," she replies.

It is an exceptionally sunny October day—one of the last brilliantly colored Rhode Island afternoons of the Indian summer, and it is the backdrop for our private beach wedding. "Ten, ten, ten—ten to the third power—it is a perfect day for our wedding," he recites in the halls of our home.

And I gleefully respond, "Yes, but don't forget it is also my birthday!" Another sip of wine, a bit of cheese and cracker, and I dab just a hint of perfume on my neck and wrist—the touch of the perfume to my skin reminds me of one of our first dates when he gently held my hand, turned it over delicately to expose the flesh of my wrist, then softly kissed it. I remember thinking he was so attentive, so loving and gentle. And now, within a few hours he would become my beloved husband.

"J.Byrd," he chimes up the stairs. "Where are you, love?" I can hear the excitement begin to build in his voice as the clock ticks forward. "I am leaving to run a quick errand and will be back," he continues.

"Okay, love, still getting ready. I love you, darling," I respond.

"I love you too." And with that he closes the front door.

One by one the girls enter the house. All dressed to the nines, they have been next door getting all dolled up for the wedding, doing each other's hair and make-up. They look lovely. My youngest is dressed in all-white with a crown of ribbon in her hair. She was the only one who was upset at the idea of the two of us getting married. It was not that she did not want us to be husband and wife, but rather that she wanted to be the one to marry him. She was admiring herself in the mirror, and I could see her imagining that this was her special wedding day too.

Two of my girlfriends arrive and surprise me in my bedroom with a few early wedding and birthday gifts. They flew all the way here to stand with me at the threshold of my new life. They had walked with me through the dark times, picked me up off the floor, and held my hands as I began to take my first new steps toward this life. I hug and kiss them and tell them how very grateful I am for their devoted friendship. One of them is raring to take photos of the family before we depart to the beach. Everyone is outside, primped and waiting to be posed for the casual photo shoot in my garden.

"It is time to go, love," he whispers. He takes my hand and leads me to the side of the house where he has discreetly hidden a black Porsche to carriage me to the beach club.

I turn to him surprised and puzzled. I had not expected a special ride to the wedding. "Was this your errand?" I ask.

"Yes." He beams, smiling, proud of himself for having delighted his bride. It is a two-seater, allowing us a few more additional precious minutes alone to enjoy the journey along the winding historic ocean highway. Hugging the curves, we take in the colorful kaleidoscope of fall leaves and deep blue sea inlets dotted with the white of boats and floating swans.

As we pull up to the beach, we can see the deck fully attended with guests from all parts of the region and beyond—a grouping of friends representing the many facets of our lives. At the top of the stairs, in a broad stance, is our preacher, a wild, loud, and cheery hippie woman dressed in a white robe and sandals. She is waving us up to start the ceremony.

He turns to me and looks lovingly into my eyes.

"Are you ready, love?" he quietly asks.

I nod yes.

I was ready; he was ready. We both were, assuredly so.

Yes, You Can Have Your Cake and the Icing Too!

On so many levels our relationship is sweet.
There is purity, honesty, beauty about who we are together.
The cake.
It is the cake, which comprises multiple rich layers.
Each a surprising, delicate, and wonderful sensation as we discover
more of each other.
The substance of our relationship.

I see a man—an honest, good, and sincere man. He is congruent.
I see a father—a devoted, loving, tender father. He is a dad.
I see a boy—the spirit of the boy within you—one who dares to explore
and experience life.

The icing.

There is passion and desire. There is love.
In your arms, I am home. Lost completely, deeply in love with you.
I am yours.

The sprinkles.

These are our shared experiences, memories, and moments
captured in time.

Red Glasses
J.Byrd Coat
Decorator Days
Pillow Conversations

New Year's
Many, many, many more we have experienced.
Many more to come.

Let's eat the cake.

Breathe.

ACT III

A Woman Undone

––––––––––

Resiliency

Clueless

The Woman at Play, Revisited

But First, My Mother

Empathy

An Awareness

The Acts of the Heroine

Pain

Letting Go of Ego

Coming to Grips

Grief

The Collective Moment

Opening Pandora's Box

Resiliency

I am not okay.

j.

Much of my research concentrates on how a little guy or gal can come back after a hard hit. Specifically, how nonprofit organizations can steady themselves in trying economic times. I am interested in not only the normal known processes, but also the ones that emerge like dandelions in the cracks of pavement. I never thought of it before, but I guess, in many ways, I am studying myself—the dandelion. I embody my research, literally.

What is resiliency? According to the Merriam-Webster dictionary, resiliency is "the ability of something to return to its original size and shape after being compressed or deformed" or "the ability to recover from or adjust easily to adversity and change." In looking back over the past twenty years, I see how either one of these definitions applies to my story. An individual's dreams and desire for growth can be compressed or deformed by another, and those who are resilient can reclaim their direction or purpose in life.

The second definition looks at "recovering or adjusting easily"— and here I step back from the definition and focus on the word *easily*. Hmm . . . rarely, I would think. In the face of adversity and change, most humans cave. The risk is high. The payout not fully known. I do agree that we can recover and adjust to adversity and change, but the definition lacks something. What about active participation? What about the ability to reframe?

According to Lester Salamon, author of *The State of Nonprofit*

America, resiliency is an organization's ability in responding and "facing enormous challenges but also important opportunities and finding ways to both with considerable creativity and resolve." In his writings he implies that although organizations respond with resilience, the act itself takes a toll on performance—even for functions of performance. Hence, not easy.

Amen.

I completely understand and agree with Salamon. It is arduous, but if you are an active player in the process, you've got a chance. It is also related to our ability for adaptive capacity—the ability to learn, respond, innovate, and motivate. Merriam-Webster, your definition needs more depth.

If asked if I had performed resiliently over these past years, I would say yes, but not to the degree I was about to face. This would be a life-and-death battle and would test the definition and me.

I am still living within this mind-space to this day. I am not okay.

Clueless

It first happened while in the university library, in the early 1990s. As I was carrying a stack of public administration books to the checkout, my arms fell open, the books tumbled out, and then slowly my arms began to curl, and my hands contorted and contracted. It was painful and I was scared. I called home panicked and asked to be picked up and taken to the hospital.

After many tests and the reviews of several neurologists, I was assured it was only a migraine that traveled outside of the head and into my body. I had suffered with all sorts of migraines my whole life. This seemed to be a good enough explanation, and I accepted it.

As time moved on and my doctoral studies continued, I would often experience little episodes in my hands along with my migraines. But it wasn't until a conference in Destin, Florida, that

I confided to my research partner that I was losing my sense of time—I was unable to remember the events of the day. When I wrote my research papers, I would swear the next day that someone else had created the work. I joked and called this mystery writer my muse. She got As, but it was very unsettling. The episodes were morphing and becoming more frequent.

In all of this medical upheaval, I had decided to take a position as a professor on the East Coast. Five months prior, my youngest daughter had nearly died. She had spiked a high fever, aspirated on her own vomit, and for several minutes left us. It was a terrifying experience—time slowed; the whole family instinctually took on roles to save her life. Luckily, when the ambulance arrived, the EMTs cleared her lungs and brought her back to us. This vivid moment in time, along with the seizures and spasms I was experiencing, plus the negative and dangerous relationship with my husband, guided me to the next chapter in our lives.

We packed.

We moved.

We divorced.

We started anew.

I saw how precious life was and how fleeting it was as well. It was time for a new life. However, my medical condition followed me and rested, for the most part, in silence. Migraines would continue, but other than that, I was clueless.

The Woman at Play, Revisited

During the "at play" point in my life, I was full of energy and would try anything new. Life would be a breath of seaside air, with trips and travels all over the planet. My marriage to Charles was in full color, and I was deeply in love. I was fearless, strong, and determined. I was working three to four jobs at a time and lecturing on multiple campuses. My mind was clicking, and my creativity blossomed.

All this energy.
Came to a halt.
One day in San Diego, California.

But First, My Mother

A few days after Christmas, five years after Charles and I were married, I received a call from my father. Mom had a heart attack, and she was in the hospital.

I dropped everything.

I wrote to my employers and said that I would need to go virtual.

I took the next plane.

My mother was extremely ill. Not only did her heart fail, but her lungs were in bad shape—years of smoking. She was diagnosed with COPD. They could not operate on her until they were able to build her lung capacity. My trip to visit her extended a week, and then another, and then another. I could not leave her.

The night before her surgery, we were alone in the room. The TV was on, and I was sitting on the edge of the bed, looking up at the screen. Mom reached over to me and tapped me. She wanted me to hold her hand—I did, but briefly. I felt my soul sink in that moment. I felt the weight of the room and the dark energy surrounding us.

"I just want to tell you how much I love you and how proud I am of you," she said.

My eyes stayed fixed on the screen. I could not turn in that moment—otherwise I would have broken down. I felt, looking at my mother—frail, ill, and frightened—that I needed to be strong for the both of us. Finally, I glanced back to her.

"I love you too, Mom."

We went silent.

The next day was surgery. My brother and his wife came to town to be of support. I remember our long wait in the room with light-blue chairs and flourescent lights, how slowly the hours passed. The surgery was a success. We would be able to see her in the morning. My brother and his wife left that very night for home—an unfortunate decision. I was staying with a dear friend of mine. She agreed to take me back and forth to the hospital as I needed. In the morning, after the surgery, my father called and asked when we would be arriving. I said we were on our way.

I brought my laptop with me so while she slept, I could work on things back home. When I arrived, she was awake and talking. She kept asking me what day it was and what time it was. I replied, "It is now 11:30 a.m." She asked where my brother was. I did not have the heart to tell her that he was no longer in town. Instead, I said, "I'm not sure, Mom." My father had taken a moment to leave the room now that I was with her. One of my mother's close friends came to visit, and in the corner of the darkened room, we whispered about her condition. I decided to walk her back to the elevator and thanked her for visiting. My father at the same moment appeared in the elevator. Together we walked back to Mom.

Something was wrong. I remember slowing our pace as we grew closer—we could hear buzzers ringing and see lights flashing outside her room. Nurses, aides, and doctors were all running down the hall. I could hear them call out her name. "Sara, do you hear us? Wake up, Sara!" A curtain was drawn, and we were not allowed in. I stood at the threshold to eavesdrop. At that moment I turned to see my father quietly standing and staring at the curtain. A clergyman came up to us to provide support. My father declined. I explained that we were agnostic, but we dearly appreciated his support.

Next in line was the "comfort-care" nurse, who asked if we would consider her services. "What services?" I asked. She explained that comfort-care was something akin to hospice. This . . . within probably ten minutes of finding Mom's room in a swirling emergency. I blurted out, "Let's give the woman a chance and a moment to heal. We don't even know what is wrong with her yet."

Dad and I walked to the seating area, dumbfounded and in a daze—we were numb.

I said I would call my brothers and let them know what was happening. I wandered down the hall to a private space and shared the news with them both. I said, "We are going to need your help." And then I returned to Dad for comfort and to provide it as well.

Not long after, the neurologist came to share an update. Mom had suffered a severe stroke. A blood clot had left the aorta and traveled to the brain, where it fractured. Multiple parts of her brain were impacted. The outcome looked bleak.

We reentered the room to find Mom on a ventilator, completely paralyzed. In the days to come she would receive tube feedings and her eyes would open, but she was trapped in a body that no longer functioned.

I remember the TV in the room being set on HGTV or the Food Network, and I wondered if she would ever again be able to enjoy her many gardens or create in the culinary arts. I thought the playing of these shows to be cruel. I changed the channel.

This was January.
Time moves forward.
It is the end of summer.

August is hot and muggy in the Midwest. The air is thick, the humidity high, and there are thousands of bugs, bugs, bugs, and more bugs. It was then that my father called me to come visit Mom in the hospital to say my goodbyes. I was to be traveling soon to New York City with my daughters, but our plans would alter, and we would reroute our trip. We visited Mom's bedside. She looked beaten and bruised, and labored for breath. She was wearing a face mask that blew air into her lungs. Unable to talk or move, she just stared beyond us, looking with a fixed gaze to the corner of the room.

My brothers showed up, one with his wife. Behind the curtain, she loudly whispered to him, "You have ten minutes, and then we are leaving." We heard every word, and I am certain Mom did too. I closed my eyes and bit my tongue, but in my head, I was screaming at her, at him, and I wanted them to leave. The day slowly unfolded as friends and family came to pay their respects. It was time to depart. She was resting quietly; the room was serene. I touched her bruised hand and whispered, "I love you."

That was the last time I saw my mother.

The next morning, my daughters and I boarded the plane for New York. We had a layover in Chicago, and it was there, in the waiting area at the gate, that I received the call from my father telling me she had passed away.

Stunned, but not surprised, the words still overpowered me. I sat still, lips tightly pursed, wondering how and when I would share this news with my daughters. At that time, the gate attendant announced that all flights were cancelled since the president was about to land. All planes were grounded until the following morning. Cots were made available to those who decided to stay in the airport, and it was here, tucked into the corner of the terminal, where I gave the girls the news. We sat in one another's arms, muffling our cries and whimpers, tears flowing.

Day One in New York City

Once we finally landed in New York City, we headed to the hotel, exhausted from our night at the airport and our grief. We arrived early and needed to wait for our room, so we sat down in the small bar area, ordered some breakfast, and the conversation began to flow. We shared stories and memories of my mom's life, not realizing that others could hear us. Two young men approached our table. One was wearing a Superman shirt. He said, "We could not help overhearing your conversation. Your loved one must have been very special. We are so sorry for your loss." As they walked away, the waiter approached, carrying a plate of chocolate-covered strawberries. "These are from the kitchen and wait staff," he said. "We are so sorry for your loss."

The belief that New York City is a hard, where kindness can't be found, is simply unfounded. We received comfort from strangers in a city, a place not our own. Once in our hotel room we again found another special package of fruit, cheese, and crackers from the hotel staff with a note stating, "We are so sorry for your loss." I lay down on the bed, wept, and fell asleep.

Day Two in New York City

The initial purpose of this trip was to see the musical *Cabaret*. I had purchased front-row tickets—spectacular. The theater was set up using tables, linens, and little lamps to give you the feeling of attending a cabaret in Germany. When I say we had front row, I mean I could extend my arm and touch an actor. We were part of the play. This musical was my mother's very favorite. She had never seen it on Broadway—yet we felt her presence. The very first note of the opening number, "Welcome," brought me to uncontrollable tears. I looked over at my daughters—waterworks. The actors obviously could see us. We wept throughout the entire performance. I do believe Mom was sitting with us.

Home

Days, weeks, and a month or two went by, and it was all a haze. Grief carried me forward to what needed to be done superficially. I was in deep mourning and without a funeral or any type of service

108

(her request), there was no closure. My heart was deeply wounded. The pain coursed through my veins.

The one thing that rested heavily on my mind was the state my mother had to endure over nearly eight months of her infliction. She was paralyzed and could not communicate, move, or eat. She was fully dependent on the care within the hospital and subsequent care centers. She was trapped. Her body was a shell of bruises. I tried my best to imagine the horror she must have felt, day in and day out. I tried my best to empathize. When she passed, there was this small sense of relief—now she was free.

Empathy

In my lectures, especially those that focus on community-oriented activity, I include one on the concept of empathy. Most of my lectures are for students who wish to be in the nonprofit or public sectors.

My lectures are based on the work of an excellent academic—you may have seen her on TV or on TED talks—Dr. Brené Brown. In one of her many videos, she defines empathy and the way it differs from sympathy (Appendix B). In short, the difference is quite distinct.

Empathy is "fueled by connection."

Sympathy is "driven by disconnection."

Theresa Wiseman, professor of applied health research in cancer care at the Royal Marsden NHS Trust in the UK, describes empathy as having four conditions:

1. Taking the perspective of others.
2. Staying out of judgment.
3. Recognizing the emotions of others.
4. Communicating that emotion.

According to Brown, sympathy is saying, "Hey, it's bad, huh?"

and then going about your way.

Empathy places you in a vulnerable state, and you connect your-self to something painful within. The result is: "Hey, I know what it is like."

As with resiliency, I thought I fully understood empathy. In my classes I use J.D. Trout's book entitled *Why Empathy Matters* (see appendix B). The concept of empathy provides a unique perspective to policymaking by considering the role of empathy or lack thereof in the process of governance. Again, through my research I thought I understood the concept, but as it would appear, not fully.

An Awareness

San Diego, California—one of my most favorite cities on the planet. I had been there countless times when I lived in Southern California. As a member of the board for a state-wide program, I was visiting the city on business. The first day, I wandered to my favorite haunts, enjoying the tastes and flavors of the region. The meeting I was attending was intense. We met in the same room for over ten hours. I spent most of that time staring at my screen, taking notes to share with others. Even our breakfast and lunch were served in this room. Over the day my eyes became weary, a migraine began to emerge, and I was simply tired. At the close of the day, 5:00 p.m., the group had set up a dinner. I declined the invitation. Instead, I wanted to find a small quiet restaurant to hide away in and rest.

Solace—an outdoor Italian restaurant, a table for one, a book on creativity and authenticity, and a glass of crisp white wine. I nestled into my chair, overhearing conversations around me, enjoying the California sunshine. But I also noticed one more thing—a slight hint of propane from the heaters on the patio. I breathed it in and considered moving tables, but in a short while I could no longer detect the scent.

As I stood up to leave, I felt dizzy and out of sorts. Walking back to the hotel, I could sense I was in trouble. My balance was off and I was disoriented. Concerned, I called a friend to talk with while I made my way back to my room. I was relieved when I arrived and thought I would take some Advil to kill the headache, but had none. I decided to sleep it off. Over the next hour, my simple migraine began to pound into my head. I really wished I had the Advil, but it would have to wait till the next day because the store in the hotel was closed.

Just before I fell asleep, my daughter called to check on me. Immediately she knew something was wrong. "Mom, are you drunk?" she asked. "No," I slurred back at her. "It's my head. This headache is out of control."

"Mom, try to sleep," she said. I agreed and turned off the TV and the lights.

A bolt of light behind my shut eyes and a crack of lightning inside my brain jolted me from my slumber. I had never felt anything so painful in my life. The pain was deep within my head, and I realized I could not sit or stand properly—the room was spinning. My first thought was, *I am having a stroke*. I crawled to the bathroom to check myself in the mirror, looking for classic signs. No. There were none. Relieved, I crawled back to bed where I once again thought I could sleep it off.

It was 1:00 a.m. I woke up lying sideways on the bed with my feet on the ground and my body and head at the end. My head was pounding, and I longed for Advil. My eyes were not focusing. The room was spinning, and my eyes were switching back and forth from tunnel vision to broken glass.

My fight-or-flight instinct kicked in—I am a fighter. I knew I needed to unlock the hotel room door, but it would be very difficult to move across the floor. I moved anyway. I reached upward. I unlocked and then slithered my way back to bed. This was an act of preservation—if I could not leave the room to seek help, I needed the maid to find me. I rested on the floor for a bit of time, trying to consider my next actions. Firecracker-like flashes of mini-headaches were happening all over my brain. I knew at this point I needed to leave the room and make my way to the elevator. If I failed, they would at least find my body in the hallway.

The hallway looked to me like a tunnel with a disappearing horizon. I crawled to the elevator, reached up, and pushed the button. When the car arrived, I climbed in. The elevator started downward to a floor where one of my colleagues entered. She looked at me. I was disheveled and obviously not ready for a meeting. I said, "Help me."

We landed on the ground level. She called out to the lobby for help. They called 911. The hospital was close by, thankfully—I could not talk much, other than a word at a time. My last sentence was, "I think . . . I . . . am . . . dying." The EMTs put me on a gurney, loaded me on the ambulance, and within five minutes I could no longer speak or move. I was trapped in my body. I could see, although at times my vision was distorted, and I could understand what others were saying, for the most part, but I was unable to communicate.

The Acts of the Heroine

I believe I had angels watching over me (thanks, Mom), and I also had angels in the flesh surrounding me. One of them boarded the ambulance. Like a heroine of myth she is legendary to me, but not to the overall populace. She absolutely possessed great strength and ability—she stayed with me for hours in the hospital and was my advocate. I admire her, and at every appropriate place and time, I exalt her achievements and qualities. She is also a central female character in this chapter of my life. I thank her from my heart for her actions.

While in the ambulance I heard a voice off to my left—a woman's voice—whispering, "I am here, and I will not leave your side." She had a British accent, and her words comforted me.

They ran an assortment of tests in the ER, wheeling me from one place to another. As I could not move my head, my gaze was straight up to the fluorescent lights and multiple doorway headers. Once again, we rolled back into my room, and I heard her voice say again, "I am here with you."

I fell asleep, and when I awoke, I experienced a sensation moving over me from the right side of the bed. I swore I felt my mother's presence. I felt her touch my right shoulder and my forehead, and then she was gone. At this moment it occurred to me that my current situation was very similar to my mother's in the months leading up to her death—paralysis, the inability to speak, the "awareness." I could now begin to empathize with her—the fear, the vulnerability. It was overwhelming and frightening.

Then, from the left side of my bed, a face leaned over me. It was my heroine, Mary, one of my colleagues from the conference. She leaned over to tell me once again, "You are not alone. I am here."

As we waited for the test results, I began to regain the ability to move my head. And then finally, I was able to speak in choppy mixed sentences and phrases. Approximately ten hours had passed in the hospital—seventeen hours including the hotel room situation.

By the time the neurologist and two of his students appeared at the foot of my bed, I was able to speak relatively well for someone who had suffered my fate. The doctor asked if the students could talk with me, because my condition was extremely rare, and they might never meet anyone like me in their career again. I agreed and explained what had happened. The neurologist diagnosed me with Bickerstaff syndrome and told me I had a unique expression of this syndrome, as the paralysis was in both sides of my body. A diagnosis—finally.

An Aside: What is Bickerstaff Syndrome? My Experience

(Note: I am not a doctor in medicine. What I am about to share with you was relayed to me over a decade of time by various doctors regarding the attempts to diagnosis my condition. This is not medical advice. Please consult your own physicians regarding your health care.) Now, with my "note" aside, what I learned about my condition is that it stems from a basilar artery migraine (also referred to as a migraine with a brain stem aura). The main artery leading through the brain stem restricts blood flow, and this affects brain functioning, which in turn produces a series of symptoms. When I experience a basilar migraine—I dislike using the word *migraine* alone here because it is not like any other of the many conventional migraines I have had—it impacts several centers. Besides producing excruciating pain that felt like sheet metal cutting through my skull, it made the muscles in my neck and shoulders feel as if they had turned to stone. In addition to sensitivity to light and sound, one of the symptoms is distorted vision. It's not like an optical migraine, where you see waves of light, broken-glass vision, or bursts and stars, lasting for only twenty minutes or so. This syndrome often produces all this, but it also includes blurry vision, the inability to see in the distance, and the strangest of all, what I call "hieroglyphic" sight, since I don't have a technical term for it. Symbols, such as letters, transform with additional lines. For instance, the letter K would have a few more lines added to it, and then it becomes unrecognizable. When this symptom first presented itself, I thought my retina was detaching and that I was going blind. I immediately went to my ophthalmologist, and during the exam, I could not make out the letters. I could see them as a new symbol but could not identify the letter as an actual letter. The doctor assured me that what I was experiencing was related to the optical nerve and my condition—not my actual vision. It was a problem of translation, of what I was seeing and how my brain interpreted the symbol. When this symptom dissipates, it either proceeds to a full-blown episode or it occurs after one is completed. This issue, in its various forms, can last for days, and my eyes physically hurt and feel strained. It takes time to recover, and this is concerning for me professionally, as I read and write for a living.

Another symptom that I experience often during an episode is the inability to speak. I generally know what I want to say, often, but no words form—I cannot produce a sound. I am mute. This usually occurs when I am fully within an episode; the hindered speech comes on slowly as full body contraction manifests. The issue of speech is also often combined with confusion—finding the right words or understanding the flow and purpose of the conversation —as well as slurring, odd responses to questions, and the repeating of phrases. This, too, has a huge impact on my work, obviously.

I also have symptoms that affect my entire body, besides paralysis, which is very painful and exhausting as I am in a contracted state. Imagine doing wall sits, as you may have done as part of sports training. In sports you may sit up against the wall for ten minutes or so, and your straining legs ache. Now imagine that for hours. That is what I feel, and the exhaustion lasts for days or weeks depending upon the severity of the episode. After the episode walking is difficult. It feels like I am on stilts, but with pain. Bending down and getting up are nearly impossible, and I need to use mobility aids to help me. After many of these episodes, I started to feel a "bubble" in my lower spine. Apparently, during paralysis your spine can compress, and over time the lower lumbar discs are impacted—causing the feeling of having a bubble lodged there. The pain and difficulty of walking, lowering and rising, are related to this symptom. Other body symptoms include numbness, painful spasms (mostly in my feet and hands), and the loss of the use of my arms either through weakness or the complete inability to move. These tell me that I am entering a basilar migraine—although it could be hours or days leading up to the event.

I also experience vertigo at times and, along with that, sustained periods of nausea. And, when fully immersed in the episode, I may move in and out of consciousness. At times this causes me to fall— often on my face. Another experience is emotional—as symptoms combine and worsen, my fear turns to anger. I lash out at people. I don't do this purposefully or with real intent; it just happens. I lose much of my short-term memory—not just moments but days and even weeks. Overall, the combined symptoms resemble a stroke, although no permanent scarring to the brain is found.

All these symptoms produce a high level of anxiety when I know an event is coming. In the back of my thoughts, I wonder if I am dying, or if I will never recover from the paralysis. This has impacted my life greatly. I have restricted my driving and try not to travel alone. I have reduced my speaking engagements, and I've moved away from lectures to an online format. I tend to not go out with friends for dinner or on excursions. I lock my phone, block numbers, or erase phone numbers altogether so I won't call or text people strange things when I am entering the event—something that used to happen quite a bit. I remain mostly at home, where I feel safe and so I am not embarrassed by my range of symptoms. At home I can, when able, write, read, cook, decorate, and garden—all the things I love and enjoy. I am basically a loner, with the exception of spending time with family and very close friends. Thank goodness I am an introvert at heart.

After I was released from the hospital in San Diego, my capabilities slowly returned—to a degree. But I was extremely drained. I craved scrambled eggs, which the hotel restaurant provided to me upon request. I know that sounds odd, but apparently it is not unusual for people with this condition to crave certain foods, such as eggs. The next day I would board a plane for home—alone. For the next several years I would endure the vicious migraines and symptoms of Bickerstaff. I went to a neurologist near us, and he confirmed the diagnosis. There is no cure, but he suggested several treatment options, from vitamins and therapy to medications or a combination of the three. I decided on vitamins and therapy as the first step. I needed the ability to think so I could continue to work and was afraid the medications would make me dull and reduce my clarity in thinking and creating.

Months later, with no improvement, I could not think—it hurt to concentrate, especially on tasks that focused on numbers. This time of my life felt dark. My memory of specific events beyond my pain escapes me unless captured on the phone and filed in the cloud. Friends started to notice my decline. One couple asked if I had gone to see Nancy, a muscular therapist. I was a little timid, as my rounds with the physical therapist had not been helpful. In fact, those sessions created new headaches on top of the Bickerstaff ones. Finally, after enduring countless migraines, I gave in and called Nancy.

Muscular therapy and massages are not the same thing. The latter relaxes and soothes. I conjure up images of scented oils, candles, and music. On the other hand, muscular therapy is at times mildly painful to agonizing. After treatment I would still feel her fingertips manipulating my knots, and I would develop bruises, but by the next day I would feel much better.

My first visit with her was extraordinary. After an hour of getting my muscles kneaded—note: Nancy was once a professional baker—I sat up in bed and noticed immediately I was no longer experiencing the pain, my constant unwanted friend. I looked at her and said, "Oh, my God, I did not realize what a no-pain body felt like anymore. It has been so long." I then burst into tears. From there I visited her on a weekly basis or sometimes multiple visits in a week. I worked with her for over a year, and although the migraines continued, her treatments provided me with some needed attention to the muscles in my neck and upper shoulders. Without her help

I fear I would have slipped back into paralysis. In between visits I would ice my head and neck with a bag of frozen peas. Reclining in a chair, I would close my eyes and try my best to relax until the cold compresses did their magic. The rotation of therapy, ice, vitamins, and ibuprofen continued over years. The times between visits decreased as I was able to manage the migraine episodes. I still had them, but now I could restrain their grip.

Pain

It wears on you. Pain.
Like a stiff tailored suit, it embraces your body.
Reaching deeper into your flesh and psyche.
It wears you down—pain.
Until you feel smaller, tiptoeing on Earth and avoiding the cracks.
It makes you numb or absent—pain is your new life.
The quality of which is diminished.
j.

Summer

During the previous spring, I noticed my youngest daughter's shoulders were not in alignment. This probably would have gone unnoticed, but I had been studying and practicing yoga at the time. I asked her to bend forward, and there it was—the severe curvature of her spinal column. Charles and I contacted a specialist and set an appointment to confirm our suspicions. We were correct—she had the S-curve type of scoliosis. We tried to correct the curve with both day and night braces, yet the curve was worsening. We decided, as a family and with our surgeon, that it was time to correct the medical issue with surgery. We would plan the procedure for early summer so she would not miss school and would have time to recover.

The day before the surgery, we went to the beauty salon to have our hair French-braided—as she would be in a prone position for some time, and the hair would mat, but more importantly this was our mommy-and-me time. I told her I was completely in this with her. Her pain was mine, and I would not leave her side. That evening, at sunset, she wanted me to take her to the lighthouse lawn so she could see the sun setting over the ocean. This was a sight to be seen. Her delicate shadow etched into the bright orange and yellow sky. I captured a photo of this brave young lady. In the morning, huddled in a small preparation room, she and I were both a mess. Thank goodness Charles was there to console us. They readied her for surgery and then turned to me and said, "You can follow us into the operation room now." I was taken aback. No one had prepared me for this, but of course I followed. The room was not very large. It was mostly white. A strange hospital bed designed for this pro-cedure lay in the middle of the room. Before they placed her under anesthesia, they asked me to lower my mask and give her a kiss. I did. My heart pounded so deeply and hard that I could hear it within my ears. I became nauseous, and I felt like the world had frozen in time. I was escorted out of surgery so they could begin the eight-hour procedure—walking down the hall felt as if I was moving through mud, and I cried deeply and profusely all the way to the waiting area. After surgery her entire spine was pinned and fused, but for of a couple of lower vertebrae.

After her spinal fusion surgery, my stress levels soared. Witnessing your child work through pain is much harder than experiencing it yourself, and shortly after surgery they had her up and walking—it was pure torture for her. Crying, screaming, yelling at me, she walked through the pain. I wept with every step. My shoulders would rise near my ears, and I would remain tense for hours, days on end. It felt as if I was continually holding my breath—my chest was tight, and I was rigid. My migraines flared. Her outcome was positive—thank God and the surgical team.

It was time to increase my visits with Nancy. At this point in my painful journey, I could take no more—therapy and vitamins were not enough. My neurologist had moved his practice, so I visited a new one, as it was time to initiate option two: medication intervention. I met with my new doctor, an interesting man—long hair in a ponytail, decked out in turquoise and silver jewelry, very quiet, pensive perhaps, who could hold a stare for a very long time while his mind worked away. He offered the same set of options as my first neurologist, plus additional vitamins, meditation, and yoga. In addition, we started a few medications that might help prevent or lessen migraines and reduce the symptoms. It was the end of summer—six years into this irritating mess.

Fall

The chimes were ringing on campus. I loved the feeling of walking through the commons at the start of the academic year. The New England air was crisp; the trees were changing into their colorful cloaks, and I was excited to meet my students. Most of my class offerings were in the library, my favorite building on campus. My office was within the graduate studies area. It was time to meet my first flock of learners. I took the stairs—three floors to the classroom. By the time I completed the first flight, I could tell I was winded. As I ascended to the second floor, my chest was tightening and as I started the third set of steps, I was completely out of breath. I could not talk. My head was pounding, and I was coughing or "barking," as the asthma symptom is referred to. I made my way to the classroom and slumped into my chair behind the desk. I motioned to the students to wait for a moment until I could compose myself. I was having an asthma attack—a serious one at that. I found this odd as exercise was not one of my triggers generally.

In trying to make sense of this episode, I thought back to the previous spring semester. During spring break, our family went to Disney World. We were joined by one of my dear friends. This was supposed to be a wild spring break for the both of us, but it was more of a broke break. My friend and I are both teachers and "wild" for us is floating in the pool and enjoying margaritas. Our second day at the park we attended the flower show. In retrospect this probably was not a good idea as I have multiple allergies. That night, after dinner, I could sense something was wrong. My chest felt heavy, and I began to "bark."

The next day we left the resort, and we traveled down the Florida coast to stay with my daughter and her family. My medical situation worsened. I lay in bed, struggling for air. My daughter rushed me to the hospital. Upon entry, hardly any questions were asked; the medical staff simply rushed me to a room. Immediately the doctors began working on me. After a few hours I was released. As we passed the check-in nurse on the way out of the hospital, she looked up from behind her computer and said, "Oh, so good to see you! I honestly did not think you were going to make it."

The next two nights we stayed with our long-time friends. By the second night, I was once again in trouble. They drove me to the nearest medical site, and again I was treated for asthma.

That same day I boarded a flight home. Charles had been monitoring my situation from afar. As soon as I landed and met him at the luggage carousel, he could see my condition was degrading. He rushed me to the ER, where I was treated and, for the first time, checked for H1N1, also known as swine flu. The test came back positive. Over the next several weeks I was in and out of the hospital. I could barely walk up the stairs at home. Over the summer the condition lingered on. I would work—light work—in my garden and then I would be fatigued. Making the bed in the morning would also do me in. I would need to lie down after doing each layer of the bedding.

Now, returning to the fall semester and my inability to climb the stairs, something still was not right. When I returned home after teaching, I was completely depleted and went straight to bed. I had another day of teaching ahead of me. When I awoke, I felt as if my heart was racing. I was agitated and uncomfortable. I thought perhaps I was just anxious and needed more rest, so I took my time dressing for work. My commute to and from the university was two hours each way. But before I set off, Charles asked if I would first see the doctor. I called our general practitioner and was told to go immediately to the hospital. I drove myself there—I do not recommend this. In retrospect, it was stupid.

It felt strange driving to and walking into the ER alone. I also felt apologetic as I thought what I was experiencing was trivial, and I did not want to waste their time. I mean, it was probably just a case of nerves and being overworked. After my initial triage assessment, I was whisked off to the back, where the doctors immediately started providing treatment. My heart rate and blood pressure were alarmingly high. My doctor, after reviewing my records, including my fight with H1N1, shared with me that he had once been a full-time pulmonologist and suspected something was wrong with my lungs, and that was impacting my heart. They took X-rays, but they revealed nothing—they looked normal. The cardiologist who viewed the test results was perplexed and ordered a stress test. The first step of the test was a leisurely walk. My heart rate and pressure immediately climbed. She ended the test abruptly—and mind you, I was on heart medication and nitroglycerin from the ER, and my heart still went nuts.

"There has to be something else causing all of this," she said. "I really think it is your lungs." She ordered a CAT scan. Meanwhile, I was taken up to my room, and it was here that I met my hospitalist. "I've been reviewing your records. You have come to the ER many times over the past year with an assortment of issues. It appears that you require a holistic approach—a team of six specialists to work with you."

An hour or so later, the cardiologist visited me to share the results of the CAT scan. "It is your lung," she replied. "Did you hit something?"

I had not.

"Then this is a spontaneous partial collapse of your lower right lung," she said. I mentioned my Bickerstaff syndrome, and she noted that it might be a contributing factor.

Shortly after, the pulmonology lab technician entered the room to provide me with steroids and a breathing treatment. She was skeptical of my illness and questioned whether she needed to treat me. I told her absolutely yes. My right lung felt as if I had a rock lodged in it. I could feel something.

She read the CAT scan results and said, "Boy, you really are sick." *Thanks for the awareness,* I thought. Before I left the hospital, I had a series of appointments set up over the next two weeks. The medical team was in place.

I will not belabor you with more details, but what I will share is that this condition has resulted in me taking twenty-five pills a day—mostly focusing on my neurological issue and lungs. By winter, a few months later, I was feeling much better. The migraines were subsiding, and my body was healing. In conjunction with what the doctors prescribed, I also decided to follow a strict diet to reduce inflammation. This helped greatly. Charles was supportive during all of it. He became my caretaker. He drove me to and from numerous doctor's appointments and checked on me throughout the day, even though it was difficult for him to be my care provider at home, especially when he had a demanding professional life. We made it through the thick and long early visits and then as time continued, the visits were spread apart, giving him what I would think to be a great reprieve.

Time Goes by, and It Is 2020—Entering the Season of Covid-19
During the months of January and February, I was teaching and traveling with Charles. I was feeling pretty good. We usually travel often during the off-season of his work life—mostly to attend conferences or meetings, but they are hosted in lovely places. Travel is something we enjoy immensely with each other. However, after one of our trips, we both came home with some type of virus. We were tested for H1N1, but it wasn't that, however much we felt like it. I was scared that I would have yet another setback in my health. It took us several weeks to recover.

In March, once again during my semester spring break, we decided to take a trip to Palm Beach and the Florida Keys. I had never been to the Keys before but had always wanted to go. During part of our stay, we visited my daughter, her husband, and our grandbaby. Since we lived so far away from them, our visits were rare, and the length of stay was never enough. After giving them kisses and hugs, we set out for the Keys. What an amazing journey. The surrounding waters looked like the Aegean with hints of lapis and turquoise. We planned to stay in Key Largo in a lovely restored historic hotel on the beach. It was charming and the community delightful. However, during our stay we learned of Covid-19, and that it had been discovered in the United States. We decided to cut our trip short, and rather than fly home, we would drive the rental car all the way up the coastline. Despite the scary news, the road trip was beautiful and enjoyable. As we passed each state, I would text family and friends our current location. One of the stops, which I pleaded to do, was Washington DC—not to stay, but as a drive through. It was cherry blossom time, and I wanted to see the pillows of pink throughout the city. Charles humored me, and we paused there to witness this beautiful spectacle. But we were in fact racing up the interstate to be sure they would not close the bridges in New York during the pandemic. A stop to see flowers was an indulgence.

Home.

Our world stopped, paused, and became barren as we clung to every word reported on this serious pandemic. Shut in, all we could do was to hope, pray, and prepare ourselves for the worst. Charles and I updated our wills and exchanged passcodes, just in case one or the other became ill and died. We blocked all friends and family from visiting our home. Both of us had conditions that might be exacerbated by Covid-19. We hunkered down.

No one wanted to get anywhere near a hospital or the ER at this time. These places were seen as virus-ridden. The doctors were attempting to understand the virus, while at the same time treating patients. Protocols to stop the spread started to be shared, and we were all on the edge of uncertainty.

It was then that my Bickerstaff syndrome began to kick into overdrive. Sitting on the couch next to my husband, I felt a thrust, a jolt of energy from my brain through my spine, and I gasped—what was happening? My spine felt alive—I was aware of the nerves running through my vertebrae. My feet felt as if they were melting or rooting into the floor. This unnerving experience traveled up my legs—heavy and fixed—and I realized that I could not move them. Downward pressure rested on my shoulders and hips, as if someone was pushing me to the ground. Next my shoulders and neck began to freeze in place and my hands started to curl. My arms then hardened. I glanced at Charles in terror. I was able to yell out, "Help me—call 911, I think I am dying!" He stood up to cross the room for the phone. When he turned back to me, I could see him through tunnel vision. It felt as if I was being sucked backward, away from him. I yelled out one more time, "I am dying!"

Before the ambulance arrived, my stepson entered our home. He is an EMT and firefighter, and he had heard the 911 call and rushed over. I looked at him with tears in my eyes and said, "Please don't let me die!" At this point I started to lose my ability to speak, but I could understand others talking to and about me. The ambulance arrived, and due to my "frozen" body in a seated position, I had to be carried out in a chair. We were off to the hospital. Due to Covid, I would have to go alone. This was a frightening thought, because I was not able to communicate, and most doctors and nurses are not familiar with this condition.

These events, during the pandemic, continued monthly from March until September. My neurologist, concerned about me being in the hospital during the pandemic, decided I would need to face these spells at home. He prescribed me an additional medication, often given to stroke victims, which would relax me through the process. It would get me out of contracture, but I was still unable to move. I was terrified. I said to him, "But I could die!" (Unfortunately, an early death is one of the many potential outcomes.) His response was, "You have not died yet, so you need to stay home and take the medication at the onset of your episode." Comforting advice? I alerted my friend, who lives out of state and is also a neurologist, of this next course of action, and asked him if it would be okay if Charles FaceTimed him while I went through the process. He agreed. When the next episode came along, my doctor friend was on the phone, coaching Charles and assuring me that I would be okay.

September—Still in the Throes of Covid-19

All courses are online.

Nonprofit had gone online.

My hair was falling out in clumps due to the medications.

I lost it.

Well, I did not see that coming—massive hair loss. I had very long, thick, brown hair. Now the texture was that of a small child's locks. I couldn't do anything about it. Frustrating, a shock to my ego, I would cry each time I brushed. I visited my neurologist to address the side effect, and a change of medication and more vitamins were added to my daily routine.

By the holidays I began to return to the "new normal." I still had an occasional migraine, spasms in my legs, arms, feet, and hands, and increased issues with my sight. But I was more alert, and I became more active—slowly. I needed *time*. Time to heal. Time to adjust. My enemy was in fact time as it related to my professional career. From the outside I looked well, but my hidden condition still had me in its hold. I further became a recluse, feeling as if I needed to wall myself away from society so I could protect myself and my career. I would retreat to my reclining chair daily, wrapped in a blanket, in my pj's, and sporting my slippers. When the pain increased, there was nothing I could do to alleviate it. Over-the-counter pain medications failed.

I would watch deadlines from work pass me by, and with that my anxiety would grow. Everything seemed to be looming over me, and my ability to learn new things was waning. I would have to concentrate so hard on the new skill, to the point where it would propel me into another episode. I found myself paralyzed in a new way—a form of fear and darkness. My family, who was also stuck with me in our house during the pandemic, was suffering from my roller-coaster emotions. I desperately wanted peace but could not find it.

During the pandemic, none of my methods of calming my mind worked. I could not muster creativity. There were several places in town I would visit regularly pre-pandemic. I enjoyed spending time in our local library—especially the fireplace room, with its leather chairs and large library tables. I could bring a project to this location and in the silence develop and complete my work. Another location, a coffee and wine bar, had multiple overstuffed couches, little niches to nestle into, and it was here that I would grade mid-terms and finals. I would also spend time on the university campus, taking walks, listening to the bells, and joining others in the commons for discussions. All these locations were no longer open—my only place was my garden and our home. I felt off-balance, as home had always been my refuge, and now it was the space where I worked all three of my positions. Life and work were seamless—it was exhausting.

Letting Go of Ego

My work schedule remained the same over these tumultuous years. I was working three part-time jobs. One, as a professor at a state university. Another, as an administrator for a state-wide program. And lastly, an executive director for a small nonprofit in my community. And, moreover, I am a wife, mother, a Mimi, and daughter. To say I was spread thin is not an exaggeration. The professional positions went virtual during the pandemic, and Zoom became a staple along with call-in phone conferences. In a weird way the impact of the pandemic allowed me to carry on in my work as my physical abilities worsened.

Just prior to the close of the nation due to Covid, I had a not-so-mini episode while teaching at the university. I became confused and could not understand the computer or my lecture prompts. I asked a student to assist me with the login, but after booting up, I remained out of it. I looked at the gathered faces of the students and said, "My sincere apologies, but I need to end class today. I am not feeling well." Surprised and confused, the students collected their things and left the room. In the emptiness of the space, I powered down the computer, pulled up the projector screen, and turned off the lights. I then wandered off toward my old office building. That space, for some reason, is my homing beacon. The building is an old New England home converted into several offices. I used to occupy an office on the second floor. I spent hours there when I first arrived on campus. I would not only work on academic work, but also personal writings. Most, if not all, of my prose and essays for "Act 1: A Woman Paused" were created there in my corner office. I viewed this space as a life saver.

On this day, I entered the main hall and collapsed on a chair. I did not have to teach again until 6:00 p.m. If I could just rest, I would be able to regroup. Joining me in the entry was another professor. He started to speak to me about the research of one of my students. I could hear him, and I knew what he was talking about on the surface, but I could not retrieve information in my brain. I just stared at him and occasionally shared some partially incoherent phrases. He took notice, either thinking I was totally out of my league of understanding or that I had been drinking. (When I go into these episodes it sort of appears as if I am drunk—slurring words, nonsense sentences, odd body movements.) My colleague switched the topic, asking me about my daughters. I was able to provide better feedback, and I quickly closed our conversation and left the office. I thought that night I could still teach. It was difficult. All my lectures are memorized, and I have taught these classes for fifteen-plus years—or more if you count other places as a guest lecturer. After class I was exhausted, my head felt heavy, and my eyes hurt.

The drive home was scary. I was deteriorating and entering the next phase. After two hours on the road, I made it home, but upon entry the full-blown episode hit, and I was paralyzed.

The reason why I share this moment with you is because this is one of many sparks of awareness that I have been collecting over several years that indicate the various changes in my life. And the aspect of change was quickening. I viewed this process with the various stages of grief. I thought I had worked so long and for so many years to be where I was in my field. I'd made all the sacrifices only to find myself sacrificed in the end. It felt like death. I could sense that I was entering the transitional phase of "ending." I dreaded this. I was depleted, and I knew that a significant amount of work and focus would be needed to move to the next phase of the "neutral zone," where the next reinvention of self would need to be conjured up, uplifted, and sustained, but in a new body—one I could not trust.

Coming to Grips

When I first moved into Charles's home years earlier, I knew it would be difficult to maintain my commute to work forever. I operated out of all three campuses and off-site locations as well. My longest commute was three and a half hours each way. The shortest was one and a half hours each way. I was not able to commute via train to these locations—I wish I could have. My only method of travel was by car.

A Loss of Independence
As I mentioned, when the pandemic hit, everything went online.

This was my saving grace, because my condition had continued to worsen and morph, with additional leg spasms and poor eyesight. I was presented with a reality—there was not a way that I could return to driving the commute. My car had over 240,000 miles on it—that is how much I had driven in a span of a few years. With the intensifying of my symptoms, I would need to limit my driving to short jaunts and refrain from interstate travel. Charles and I decided to purchase a new car, one to share—mostly so he would feel comfortable driving me around if needed. I look back at this moment as a process of coming to grips with reality. I now needed to rely on others for any travel beyond the scope of our small town. I was becoming dependent.

A Loss of Community and Friends

And another blow, when I have these episodes, prior to not being able to speak—I am often hateful and hurtful with my words. I ramble—often incoherently. I do not remember any of the time within the episode, but my victims do. Many realized that I was in a different state of mind. To protect myself and others around me, I would self-isolate—a hermit staying put on a plot of land within the confines of my home. I went as far as to clear my contacts from my phone so I could not speed dial friends. I created barriers, checkpoints, so I would do as little harm as possible.

A Loss of Physical Attributes

I had mentioned my appearance—hair loss. When I first shared this with close friends, in their thoughtful way to comfort me, they would say, "You will look great in a scarf!" or, "How fun, you can wear wigs!" At first that wasn't what I wanted to hear, but months into not being able to style my hair, I decided to purchase hair pieces—buns, ponytails, etc. I loved them, especially on days when I just needed to get up and run to the next appointment. I was taking a regimen of vitamins and using special shampoos and conditioner, and yes, my hair slowly but surely was coming back.

A side effect of some of my medications was weight gain. My neurologist friend gave me a warning that it was not unusual for many, on one drug, to gain forty to fifty pounds. I did. Since I am no longer on the medication, the weight has come off, but it was unsettling and expensive as I had to purchase new clothes.

Another fun item in the appearance category—again, I wasn't prepared for this—was the damage to my teeth. Some of the medications created a very dry mouth, and even though I was following proper dental practice to improve this, I still fractured two teeth and broke another in one week. I literally felt like I was falling apart.

A Loss of Profession and Personal Attainment

One area that I did not want to alter but needed to were elements of my career. I mentioned not being able to drive the commute, but I also needed to let go of several of my projects. For me, to be able to produce new works on unfamiliar concepts, I needed to be able to go into a trance-like state and stay there to create. I needed to be able to "see" into my brain for the structural components of my work and how they paired with theories related to my field. With my condition, after experiencing an episode, much of my short-term memory is erased. To continue my work, I would need to reread everything to find the spot where I had left off and to understand how I wanted to take the work forward. The disability office did not know how to serve my needs. What I needed was more time. Not test-taking or note-taking time, or various services, but time itself (extensions). I became so frustrated that I released my projects and stepped away. I was done. This was a costly move and would directly alter my future, but it needed to happen. The aggravation and embarrassment were too much. The stress it produced created a vicious cycle of related episodes. I cried a lot over this decision as my work persona was an identity I enjoyed and took pride in, but now I realized it was not the door I was to keep open any longer. I needed to and am in the process of creating a new type of professional life—one where I can control time.

Grief

WebMD contributors Dr. Jennifer Casarella, MD, and Debra Fulghum Bruce, PhD, point out that when you lose someone or something dear to you, it's natural to feel pain and grief. "The grief process is normal," they write, "but when grief takes over your life, and you begin to feel hopeless, helpless, and worthless, then it's time to talk to your doctor about telling the difference between normal grief and depression." They point out that grief is a natural response to death or loss. The grieving process is an opportunity to appropriately mourn a loss and then heal, and it helps when you acknowledge grief, find support, and allow time for grief to work.

Before I moved into my career of teaching political science, I worked in the gerontology department. I taught classes related to the aging process, and grief was one of the concepts discussed. I would share with students Elisabeth Kübler-Ross's five stages of grief: denial, bargaining, depression, anger, and acceptance. (Appendix B.)

Death does not necessarily mean death of the body—it can also mean death or loss of a persona, role, identity, or relationship. I experienced this when my ex-husband and I were divorced, when I made a drastic move away from my support network, and when I changed my place of employment. Change is hard, but it is constant. I can teach this to my students, but that doesn't mean I do not feel or go through these difficult stages myself—I am aware enough to recognize them, but I am usually a hot mess while moving through them.

The Collective Moment

All the aforementioned led me to what felt like the "unpeeling" or the "undoing" of self. I continue to remind myself to reframe the situation from loss toward growth. As an avid gardener, I am constantly creating new beds, but I also change those that are no longer thriving. I do not get mad at the plant for not producing leaves or blooms; instead, I consider a new environment for this form of life. I give it fertilizer (nourishment), water (cleansing and replenishing) and enrich the soil (grounding). But most of all, I give it *time* to take root. The newly planted in their first year sleep, in their second they creep, and in the third season they leap.

Why wouldn't I do this for myself?

I am here, the environment no longer suits, it is time to replant, take root so that I may thrive.

This does not mean a full alteration, but instead a deeper look at which facets are no longer viable. (It begins with an ending. Appendix A.)

The reckoning did not rapidly appear, no. In fact, I blocked it by trying my best while at my worst and continued my same behaviors, but in a different body—one that was calling to rest. I began to take the time to consider what I truly loved to do. I am content in my current surroundings. I quietly move through the day, paying close attention to the little stuff, as would a painter or poet. These creative acts feel like I am sculpting my life. I love this space and it inspires me. (The Neutral Zone, appendix A.) I am searching.

Earlier this year, after our vaccinations, Charles and I took a road trip to Vermont. We stayed in a historic hotel built several years before the American Revolution. The hotel was nestled in a valley between the green rolling hills. The entire town felt like a snapshot of history. What I noticed, as we made this pilgrimage, was the number and variety of artisans creating throughout the state. I could understand why—it is beautiful and lush. Covered bridges and little townships dot the state. It is a magical space. The creative communities inspired me, and during our visit, time stood still for a moment, or two, or three. My soul was recharging, and a bit of clarity was entering my mind.

I can already sense that this year the transformation will begin. There are natural endings for most things, and I am allowing them to develop at their own pace—making space for new opportunities to arise by letting go of those elements that no longer suit.

On the horizon are the next steps.
I am ending . . . with a new beginning.
I have much left undone.

Love,

j.

P.S. Time to bake a new cake.

Full Stop
What you have come to believe about your health has been misguided.
Not by malice or malpractice, but by mimicry.

Back to the Haystack in Search of the Needle
Stunned silence.

Charles and I had both sat there in this sterile room with the doctor apologizing for his information, but at the same time he was forcing a reality. The condition, although not a fatal diagnosis, was one that medicine could not cure.

I said nothing.

I just stared into the doctor's eyes.

I took my right-hand thumb and finger and pinched my left hand with all my might so it would render me silent.

I needed to hear. Not think. Hear.

Toward the end of his soliloquy, which was dotted with references to men's inability to have erections—what the hell? But apparently there is a link between that and what I now have . . . for the love of God—he said, "I know you are upset and probably mad, but there are few doctors who would say this to you because they have not seen enough cases or have had the span of years of practice to do so—we can't do anything for you but help you cope."

After a few breaths I reached over to him. Touched his hand. He had read through the decades of files and decided that I had been misdiagnosed all these years, and all the medications I had been taking were not helping, nor could they. In fact, they were making me physically and emotionally sick. I was zombie-like and would throw up all the time.

I finally opened my mouth and said, "Thank you. Weirdly this is a good thing, I think. I traveled to you for a different perspective, and you provided it. Thank you for taking the time to review and comment. Now I can move forward."

He touched my hand.

I won't die from this condition, not directly at least, and it also means I am not on all the medications I'd been previously prescribed. I am on zero. I went from twenty-five pills a day to nothing. Talk about detoxification. My insides have been damaged a bit because of the previous years and other factors, but now I am on a new path.

However, in the aftermath of this doctor's visit, Charles and I left the office, jumped into an Uber to Katz's Deli, where the shock finally wore off and I burst into tears over my plate of the World's Best Pastrami Sandwich. Thank God for good food.

So, I am back to the needle in the straw—I found it, but now I need to understand it and deal.

The Views From Here Are Spectacular

I was at a delightful lunch looking over a vineyard in California. Perched high above, you could see for miles. I love this part of the state—truly. We both ordered Cobb salad and iced tea. The conversation started, cleansed and practiced. I had met her only once before—she is a delightful force of a woman. Partway through the salad she asked a question from an observation and perhaps a slight comment from me the night before. "You mentioned that you could not eat most of your dinner last night as you were not feeling well." I replied with a yes. She responded, "I notice you are doing the same thing today at lunch. Are you okay?" And then I confessed my situation to her.

The night before I almost did not have dinner with them. When we arrived, after the flight and then a very long drive from the airport, I was ill. Motion is not a good thing for me. When I go on a trip, I need to prepare to be sick. But I love to travel and refuse to let go of this pleasure. We had arrived in a black Suburban. It was comfortable, and I sat in the front seat, but regardless, I was "sea" sick.

By the time we arrived at the winery, I was shaking—then throwing up. I took to bed and stayed there until our reservation time. Charles asked if we should cancel. "No! I will make it through. I did not fly across the country to sit in this room." During the last minutes I cleaned up and we went.

"I almost did not have dinner with you," I responded to my lunch partner. "I have some type of neurological thing, but I am here now, and the views from here are spectacular. Thank you for the lunch invitation." She inquired about my condition, and I provided a cursory response. She then looked at me as if she'd heard me. "I know someone in New York City whom you must see. I will arrange it," she said. As we drove down the mountain back to the vineyard she told me, "This is serendipitous. Our meeting. Our lunch."

I agreed.

Awakening

"What you have been told and treated for is all wrong."
"You should not be on any of that medication."
"You have been misdiagnosed."
"Never go into an ER again for this condition as they may kill you—
they won't understand what is happening to you."

A New Direction

I went to New York City and met with the neurologist. I had sent him all my files from the previous years and medical institutions. After meeting with me and sharing the news regarding my condition, he suggested that I meet with one of his colleagues. I made my next appointment. I have a feeling that this was a double-check on the New York medical evaluation—the second confirmed. I have functional neurological disorder (FND). There is no disease associated with this disorder, but it produces weakness, movement disorders, blackouts, seizures, spasms, paralysis, sight issues, loss of or slurred speech, neuropathy, and short-term memory loss. The best description that I have seen contrasts FND with MS and other similar diseases, which impact "brain hardware" and leave physical damage. FND is a "brain software" issue—parts of my brain were not communicating with each other, or there was some type of brain development issue. The symptoms present themselves like the other diseases and create the same physical responses, but do not leave permanent damage. The fix? Coping and pain management. I leave the meeting unsettled, confused, and intrigued. The second doctor, the colleague, again reiterated, "Do not go to the ER—they will harm or kill you. They will not understand what is happening to you and they will perform tests or procedures that could permanently— let me say this again—harm you or kill you. Stop going to all your other doctors. If there is a situation call me." Wow, okay. I told him that it had really almost happened. I was given a spinal tap, and it did not seal properly. The nurses moved me too early. I ended up in bed, lying flat on my back for weeks, moaning like a dying animal, and developed a severe spinal headache because of this test.

His last word to me was, "See?"

Next Steps

Step One: Learn to deal with and understand this reframing of my condition.

Step Two: Continue to work with my new doctors.

Step Three: Learn how to manage my pain using a variety of techniques (yoga, meditation, and a variety of therapies)—back to the original plan from years ago.

Step Four: Learn how to cope. I look at this coping in two ways. Spiritually, as I feel like I have lost time, having been robbed of time on all the medications and their side effects. I was dull, listless, distracted, highly agitated, frustrated, and constantly feeling ill. I lost moments with my family; I was not fully present in my work; I had to let go of people, studies, and careers I loved. This will take some time, but therapy will help. Physically, I need to cope, but in the sense of detoxification. Coming off all those medications was a ride. I need to repair my body—inside and out. I started this work recently, and it has had a profound impact. My skin, my hair, my nails, my lymph nodes, my organs, my blood flow—all impacted by the toxins that I took in over several years.

Step Five: Repair my relationships and allow the next path in my life to emerge. And then fall into it.

Step Six: Listen and trust the new team of doctors, therapists, and specialists.

Step Seven: Love Charles with all my heart for sticking with me through this.

Psyche Opening the Golden Box, John Williams Waterhouse (1903)

Opening Pandora's Box (Jar)[1]

Everyone has a Pandora's box in their lives. The difference between people is whether the individual chooses to peek inside—revealing the evils in one's life—and whether they choose to share this side of themselves with others. Each of us decorates our boxes and disguises them well. They are personal, raw, real, and bare the soul. Some may know the contents of their personal boxes, and others may never wish to recognize these aspects. There are various reasons for this suppression, and they depend on social status, age, race, gender, life circumstance, economics, etc. When someone takes the time to purposefully and intensely deconstruct their lives, find their inner selves, recreate their life world, and dare to open the box, it is a traumatic and life-altering event. If and when contents are shared with those individuals most loved and trusted, it is a gift of the heart. Others around them, especially those who dare not to look at themselves, are not only confused by this inner journey that one undertakes, but also are surprised by the contents and question what is being revealed. It is for this reason, the questioning, that many

---

[1] From jar to box, the original writing, "Works and Days," by Hesiod, was translated into Latin from Greek. In that translation, by Erasmus, jar was replaced with box. (*Pandoras's Jar: Women Greek Myths,* Natalie Hynes, 2020)

choose not to share or seek guidance in dealing with these evils. However, for those who move forward and face the demons and the questions from friends with raised eyebrows . . . there is hope.

Pandora, when opening the box and thus releasing all its evils onto mankind, closed the box just before the last item could be released—that item being hope.

What I have shared with you about my life has been hidden in my Pandora's box. The sharing of its contents is not intended to fix anything, seek retribution, convince anyone, or scar or hurt anyone more than it already has—the contents are simply being released to the winds so only hope remains. By releasing them I take away their power. Note: these evils do not define me; by letting them go, I have reclaimed my life.

Epilogue

A Letter to Mom: Criss-cross, Circle, Kiss

On January 2, 2014, my mother underwent open-heart surgery. The next day she suffered a stroke—a single blood clot had exited the heart after the procedure (where it most likely formed from the clamp), traveled to the brain, and shattered into multiple fragments. For months she lay in various states of responsiveness and endured many additional assaults to her body: a punctured lung, several respiratory infections, multiple intubations, and a tracheotomy. Her determination and will to live was not only impressive, but heroic. My mother had always been a salty woman, but underneath she was soft and vulnerable. Her crusty exterior was a front used to protect and deflect people from knowing her, judging her, and harming her. Her ability to fight through this medical trial altered my view— she was indeed brave, strong, and determined. My respect for my mother deepened, and I was humbled.

I remember my first thought of realization regarding her condition as I sat stunned in the back seat of our friend's car leaving the hospital on that first night—I wanted my mom back.

I missed her voice. I missed talking to her.

There were so many things that I still wanted to say to her. This thought continually played in my head days after the surgery. You always hear people saying this line at times like this to the point where it seems a cliché. But now I know that it is not. It is a truthful statement, and it is a sad reality. There were things I should have uttered on the days leading up to her surgery but could not. These words were somehow lodged in my throat and stuck on my pride. I told myself that I had a role to play in the hospital. Dad was there to hold her hand and calm her. My daughters were there to hug and kiss her. I, on the other hand, felt the need to be the badass checking on the nurses, questioning the doctors, reducing her fears through my display of being strong, in control, and organized. I was determined to will her through this scary time by wearing a cape of confidence.

She wanted in. She wanted to hold me and break down, I could tell. Instead, I told her to concentrate and focus on the process that would increase her lung capacity before the surgery. I urged her to spend her time practicing breathing into the plastic tube and moving the ball up the pipe. "Focus, Mom. Now is not the time to worry. You need to think positively and focus. You have a fight ahead of you."

The night before surgery, she reached her arm out across the bedside table. "I know nothing will go wrong, but I just want to say . . ." she started. I turned to her. ". . . I just wanted to say that I love you. And, that I wanted to be a good mother. I wonder if I was a good mother. I was not perfect, and I apologize for not being perfect. And . . ." she said.

I interrupted and coolly responded, "You are a very good mom. You were a great mom. I have no bad feelings or bad memories about you at all."

"I just wanted to say that I am sorry if I was not and that I tried my best and . . ." she repeated.

Again, I interrupted. "You were wonderful. My childhood was wonderful. I could not be the woman I am today without you being wonderful. It will be okay. I am here." I said this as if we were making out a grocery list or something—with a matter-of-fact voice, the reading of lines, and lacking passion. *What the hell is wrong with you?*

I thought to myself. *Get up and move toward her.* I never moved from the chair. I never even moved in the chair. My body was still and hardened by fear. A small stream of tears flowed from the corners of my eyes, but my face remained stoic. I looked at her, and she turned back to me for a short moment. "I love you, Mom," I said.

She retracted her hand—the hand that I never reached out to touch. I turned back to the TV—never really watching, just staring, wishing this was all a very bad dream. If I could go back in time to that very moment . . . what I wish I would have done:

I would have immediately risen from the chair. I would have reached out to her extended hand, held it, and kissed it. I would have done our "good luck" kiss to her hand—a criss-cross pattern with a circle drawn around it made with my fingertip and then a kiss in the middle for good luck.

That was my secret good luck sign I would make on her hand when I was a little girl. I would do this when she got ready to go to bingo with her girlfriend Linda. She would be all dressed up in a tight turtleneck sweater and plaid bell-bottom pants, wearing square-heeled patent shoes and a long chain necklace—usually the one with a big gold jewel-eyed owl hanging from the loop. Her hair was always spoofed up, "ratted" was what she called it, and she smelled like perfume. Maybe it was the expensive perfume, Joy, that she bought on her trip to Europe—the same bottle of perfume on her dresser that I had opened without permission and accidentally knocked over, spilling half onto her table mirror. I remember standing at the front door, asking for her hand so I could make the good luck sign. She would extend it, palm up, toward me. I remember her long painted fingernails and the big turquoise-and-silver rings on her fingers as I clutched her hand and began to draw *criss-cross, circle, kiss.*

If I had held her hand, I would have noticed that her nails were very long and that they were not painted and that she was not wearing rings. I would have noticed that she had removed her wedding ring, fearful that they might have to cut it off. I would have quietly, lovingly, and tenderly said to her, "You are a wonderful mother and grandmother. You are such a good mom. It will be okay. We are here with you. We love you so very much. You are so very loved. You will be safe. We are here to protect you. We love you." And then I would have hugged her. I would have hugged her so tight, she would have gasped. So very tight she would have felt how deeply I loved her—my heart pounding, the warmth of my body. There would have been no doubt as to how much I loved her. None.

Luckily there were other moments later in the day and on the morning of her surgery when I was able to hold her hand, hug and kiss her, and do the *criss-cross, circle, kiss*. But that one private and defining moment I want back. I want it back so that there could be no doubt. No doubt as to how much I love and adore this woman. I love you, Mom . . .

Criss-cross,

j.

A Love Letter to Charles

Through decades of time,
Over 1,382 miles
Across state lines and adventures around the planet, I searched.
I knew you were there—somewhere.
I knew that I would know in an instant when I found you.
A leap of faith carried me in your direction. Blind faith.
I saw your face, and I paused.
We are masters of our fate, you say. I agree.
I steered my boat toward your coastline.
I opened my heart and you entered.
I allowed myself to love again—you did too.
It was as if I had known you my whole life, and we went forward from
where we left off in conversation.
You held my hand—I knew you.
Together now through the decades of time, we have traveled thousands
of miles together.
Exploring hand-in-hand.
I am home with you wherever we go.
You. Are. Home. To. Me.
I love you,

j.

Wherever We Go—I Am Home With You

The New York Hilton, Marriott World Center, Shingle Creek, Marriott Marquis San Diego Marina, Hotel Del Coronado, the Ocean House, Hilton Hawaiian Village, the Kahala, Turtle Bay, Aulani, the Mount Washington Inn, the DoubleTree in Augusta, GA, the Marriott in New Orleans, LA, the Belmond Hotel, the Kiawah Island Resort, the Jupiter Beach Resort, the Dolphin and the Swan, Animal Kingdom Lodge, Wilderness Lodge, the Beach Club, Marriott Marquis in San Francisco, CA, the Beauport Hotel, the Broadmoor, Fairlane Hotel, the Gaylord Palms, Aloft in Delray Beach, FL, Bakers Cay Resort, Casa Marina, the Seaport Hotel, the Equinox, the Harasekett Inn, the Moana.

My Four Little Women

When Amy was born, a friend of the family's said to me, "Oh, look! You now have the Little Women in your home!" I was pleased to hear this and a bit dismayed that I had not already come to this same conclusion earlier. "Yes, you are right, I do!" I responded. And this literary comparison is perfect. My little women have loved the book and movies since they were very young. When we moved to the East Coast, we visited the Alcott home in Concord, Massachusetts. It was a time capsule. Louisa May (aka "Jo") made a handsome income from the publishing of her books and was able to preserve most of the family's personal belongings. She filled the Orchard House with these, and it later became a museum. I was struck by one item most of all—her writing desk. It was an extremely small, wall-mounted desk underneath her bedroom window, not large enough for a small laptop—I'm surprised it fit paper and quill. It was here the docent explained that Louisa May wrote the entire 759 pages of *Little Women* in under three months.

The writing of my book took many years of collecting short stories, prose, and poetry. But, when I sat down to write the book, I was reminded of Louisa May and her three-month writing timeline. I decided during the pandemic to do the same. Each month would be a section. I would write it over a summer when I was most alone in the home. And you know what? It poured out of me.

Now back to my little women. I tried not to write their stories within mine. Each of my girls is a very talented writer, and talented in multiple areas of the arts. They have their own voices, so I have no reason to supersede. But being Marmee, I do want to share where they are now—beyond the turmoil that they, too, endured by my side.

Meg (my oldest)

My first sweetheart. You have excelled in theater and the arts throughout your college years. Upon graduating in the US, you decided to attend the University of Birmingham's Shakespearean Program in Stratford-upon-Avon, UK—the home of the dear bloke. I enjoyed watching you walk across the stage when you earned your master's degree, and now you are finishing your doctorate. Bravo!

Jo (my second oldest)

My little Jo. You completed your degree in cultural anthropology, became a published author, and have since married and have given us the next generation of Marches. Your understanding of others, along with your ability to discern wine, coffee, and tea has led to your current position in working with extremely private clubs in some of the loveliest places in America. I enjoy watching you move forward in your graduate work at Harvard University. Well done you!

Beth (once the baby, but now my third-born)

Dear one, much like Alcott's Beth, you have an open loving heart, and you are an artist, especially one of confection. You have studied at the top culinary school in the United States and your abilities in pastry are extraordinary. You have a lovely family and a little one, a sweet flower of a child. I see you beam when you look at your bloom. I am so proud of you!

Amy (the baby)

Sweet baby. Deep thinker and intense artist, your abilities astound me. I cannot wait to see where your academic pursuits take you. You were accepted into one of the top fine arts programs in the United States. Like with Amy in *Little Women*, your art fills our home. The world is open to you. You're a newlywed, and while completing your studies and developing your art, you'll be starting a new life adventure, exploring the world with your husband and kittens. I see colors around you—perhaps it's my synesthesia at play. Your work is thought provoking, intelligent, and I cannot wait to go to your first solo opening!

Appendix A

Navigating the Spaces in the Meantime

Transitions

I have a favorite book from college entitled *Managing Transitions: Making the Most of Change* by William Bridges (Addison-Wesley, 1991). This book has been a useful guide in my life as its message has served me well in dealing with several of life's issues—including those with my ex-husband. The book was introduced to me over twenty years ago by my late mentor, a professor in gerontology, and her core message was that life is in a constant state of change, and as a result we are given opportunities to transition—to grow and develop. And it is our job to pay attention, reflect, and act.

For a successful transition to take place, it is important to understand that transition can be described as a three-stage cycle: stage one is an ending, followed by a period of transition, and then concluding with a new beginning. For a transition to be meaningful, rather than doomed in a cycle of repeat, the ending should be acknowledged. The transitional process (otherwise known as the unknown or "neutral zone") should be embraced, allowing the individual to make a well-considered choice, resulting in a purposeful start, a beginning.

The middle of the transitional process, the period of the "neutral zone," is the most important phase of the cycle. It is here where growth, discovery, and creativity take place for the individual. In our society, however, the walk through the neutral zone is often shortened to a sprint, as people feel the need to have things done *now*, and in the immediate. Not only are we compelled to quickly "fix the problem," others around us—onlookers—can be uneasy with the timing and pace of the unknown, and as a result they often attempt to hurry the transitional process. The task for the individual, within what appears to be a contemplative phase, is to allow it to unfold at its own rhythm. And for *you*, the participant in the process, the task is to simply breathe, reflect, and consider your options while acting. Mostly, this means figuring out how to be comfortable in living with the unknown, and yes, I realize this is a tall order. But it is necessary to the process.

Resisting the transition or ignoring it leaves one fixated or stuck. And for me, my stuck-ness appeared in the form of sleep-walking -through-life behaviors in my marriage. I was there, but I was not present. I saw myself in pictures at events, holidays, and celebrations, but I had little to no recollection of the experience. I was simply there in the physical form—smiling, nodding, and participating in chitchat.

I strongly resisted entering the transition. I was not willing to move forward, as I felt doing so would mean giving up and losing all I had—you know, the crap that you accumulate over years of marriage, the fantasy of growing old together in retirement, and so forth. So, in dealing with the meantime I would stall the movement. I was guilty of filling in the holes of my life with things, education, food, wine, friendships, outings, and work so as not to live life, but to cover it up under the layers.

Interestingly, but not surprisingly, once I had committed to starting the process by ending the relationship and changing my life, others around me were confused and afraid and wanted me to give up this venture. I was accused of being self-centered, a "bad" mother for leaving their father, and being one of those "career-oriented" women (whatever *that* means). When these same people discovered the intimate details of the situation, however, they were quick to run with me into the neutral zone but were also the first to prompt and prod me to rush through it as well.

"You really need to hurry up and divorce him!" they would exclaim.

"What are you waiting for? You are not going back to him, right?" they would taunt.

"I really think she will stay with him or why else would she drag her feet?"

I resisted their pushes and pulls.

I was acutely aware of where I was in the process—now awake, I was very present in my life.

I was in transition.

I had become a woman paused.

They were not aware of the thousands of moving parts that encompassed this transitional process—some legal, some emotional, and some financial. The process had its own timetable. I had entered the neutral zone, and believe me, I was uneasy. I too wanted the uncertainty over. I wanted him out of my life. I wanted to collect child support for crying out loud (which later I would find to be the biggest joke of all and the most revealing about him, his family, and our justice—or injustice—system). But all those wants had to develop at their own speed. Whether or not others could understand or support my actions was beside the point. I simply did not care.

The point of being in the neutral zone is for *you* to do what needs to be done so that *you* have the ability to take the best course of action—to start *your* new beginning. The beauty of this transitional space for me was that it allowed me the time to evaluate my identities, grasp the situation fully, clear my head and heart of the pain and anguish, and begin to act rationally, purposefully, and strategically.

Grieving and Uncovering the Self

I was not fully prepared for the numerous losses involved in the process of transition—to change your life in this manner is to give up a multitude of aspects of one's life in exchange for another. I fully expected losing material possessions, some shared friendships, and a certain level of lifestyle—mostly I was prepared for the obvious losses. But I had not expected the profound losses of known personal identities—not just one, but the multiple roles one assumes across a lifetime.

I soon discovered that when change propels you into this process, an examination of each assumption of the self occurs within the different spaces that we occupy. It is a self-reflective, introverted process, Bridges points out, resulting in the letting go of roles that no longer fit within this new life. We shed them to embrace new ones. The letting go is the hard part. Saying goodbye to an aspect of the self triggers an associated mourning process with the passing of each identity. In fact, it is very similar to Kübler-Ross' stages of grief. The stages (denial, anger, bargaining, depression, and acceptance) can occur after any form of catastrophic personal loss, and result from an inability to change the situation. The situation does not need to be a negative one, just an experience that significantly alters one's life. These stages do not follow any specific order, nor does a person have to experience all stages to move through grief. But resisting movement between stages results in individuals "sticking and cycling" to avoid the grieving process.

The mourning process is slow and tedious. Bridges mentions the stages of grief in his work also and discusses them in terms of the loss of identity. Eventually I had come to anticipate the grief cycle and realize that with release of an image of the self there came the discovery of a newly acquired role—and these aspects were stronger, more true, vibrant, alive, and most importantly, congruent with my core being. I was not transforming into someone else; I was rediscovering myself.

Surprisingly, there came a point during the transition when I learned to engage in the process, even anticipating the prospect of discovery. I found that certain aspects of the self were easier to let go of than others. Some of the most learned and beloved identities I tightly clung to, but eventually, I quietly and solemnly released them, one at a time.

Reflecting on my personal writings, I found that I could group aspects of identity into "spaces" in my life—physical, cultural, relational, and intellectual. I navigated the movement through these spaces and into the neutral zone. My writings are a reflection of my experience—it centers on this important and uncomfortable stage of the transition. The moments of pause.

Some Additional Insights on Pausing

"When a great adventure is offered, you don't refuse it."
—*Amelia Earhart*

Reframing

At some point in the process, I came to view the action of transition as an adventure. It was my attempt to reframe the situation into one that I could bear. I would share this reframed view of my life with my daughters to aid them in letting go, picking up, and moving on within their own lives. I would tell them, while at the same time trying to convince myself, that now, in that moment, we had been given the opportunity to create our lives, purposefully. We could become anyone, with no familial ties or friendships to define us in specific roles, no barriers. I would ask the girls to dream. I would repeat to them, when I would see them fall into old traps from our past life, that we were no longer in the Midwest, and that "Our house is one of peace." These became our mantras, to keep us moving, discovering, and pushing ourselves to become and uncover ourselves.

Informal Associations (Friends, Family, and Colleagues)

What I also came to discover was that I was not alone in the process. Yes, much of what you encounter in transition is internal, but what helped me climb over each wall and supported me in facing my fears, were others in my life—a few friends, colleagues, and family members. As the situation unfolded, I would share my story. I watched and listened to the reactions of those around me. Many quietly supported, others stepped away, and then there were those few who stood next to me, sometimes leading in front of me. These few, wildly brave, outspoken, and ferocious people were those who believed in me. They saw *me*. They saw me even when I did not see myself. They heard me even when I did not realize I had called out. These individuals, to whom I am forever in deep gratitude, were vital to my transition process. A secret ingredient in managing a personal transition is to surround yourself with those who believe in you, who say yes, who are cool with risk, and who reaffirm your movements—supporting you in rediscovery of the self.

Surround yourself with mirrors, which reflect who you want to be. Discard those who do not cast reflections that aid you in your journey. Now is not the time for criticism, but for clarity and for praise.

Modeling Behavior

Beyond reframing and surrounding yourself with believers, it is also helpful to model the successful behavior of others who have managed transitions well. I did not have a mentor to follow. No one in my close circle of friends and family had negotiated something like this, and lacking a real-life role model, I looked to other sources: movies, books, and music. When I first started watching and reading stories of other strong, determined, ambitious, and adventurous women (and some men) facing adversity, I was not aware that I was using them as models. I was simply drawn to their stories. I studied them. I would watch movies or documentaries about them, sometimes multiple times, and read books of their personal accounts. I even met one of the authors. Eventually I came to understand my obsession with their tales—they were my path blazers.

Here are some of the stories that inspired me, in no particular order:

Films
Out of Africa
Under the Tuscan Sun
The Bridges of Madison County
Chocolat
Miss Potter
The Age of Innocence
Contact
Cinderella Man
A Beautiful Mind
Little Women

Books
Out of Africa (and related biographies), by Isak Dinesen
Under the Tuscan Sun, by Frances Mayes
The Bridges of Madison County, by Robert James Waller
Reviving Ophelia: Saving the Selves of Adolescent Girls, by Dr. Mary Pipher
The Last Lecture, by Randy Pausch
The Invitation, by Oriah Mountain Dreamer
The Dance, by Oriah Mountain Dreamer
Managing Transitions: Making the Most of Change, by William Bridges
Little Women, by Louisa May Alcott
A Year by the Sea, by Joan Anderson

Music
Norah Jones
Alanis Morissette
Sting
Carrie Underwood
Anna Nalick
Enya

Appendix B

More on Empathy, Depression, and Grief

Resources on empathy

Trout, J. D. *Why Empathy Matters*. Penguin Books, 2010.

Brown, Brené. "Brené Brown on Empathy." Accessed September 10, 2024. youtube.com/watch?v=1Evwgu369Jw.

Brown, Brené. "Shame & Empathy by Dr. Brené Brown." Accessed September 10, 2024, https://www.youtube.com/watch?v=qQiFfA7KfF0.

Brown, Brené. "Brené Brown on the Power of Vulnerability at TEDx Houston 2010." Filmed December 23, 2010 in Houston, Texas. ted.com/talks brene_brown_the_power_of_vulnerability?subtitle=en.

In the videos listed above, Brené Brown, a renowned researcher in the field of social work, discusses vulnerability and empathy. She describes the difference between empathy and sympathy and talks about vulnerability and the willingness to be open.

The Stages of Grief

In *On Death and Dying*, her seminal work from 1969, Swiss-American psychiatrist Elisabeth Kübler-Ross describes grief as typically being made up of five stages, namely denial, anger, bargaining, depression, and acceptance. In later editions, she points out that the stages do not necessarily occur in a specific order, and that not everyone experiences all five stages.

Denial may also present as numbness or shock and is a normal reaction that helps to protect us from the intensity of feeling at first.

In the bargaining stage, thoughts are dominated by what you "could have" or "should have" done to avoid the loss. This can be a very distressing, confusing time, and may lead into feelings of guilt and anger. Anger itself is often a smokescreen for sadness or confusion. Sometimes anger is directed at the person who died (because we feel abandoned), a higher power, or at the doctors. A lot of anger comes from feeling helpless. In the depressive phase we also find ourselves feeling helpless as the full extent of the loss sinks in, and we might feel lonely, anxious, and without purpose.

Finally, acceptance comes once we have processed our emotions around the loss, and this is when healing can begin.

Resources

Kübler-Ross, Elisabeth. *On Death and Dying*. Scribner reissue edition, 2014.

Fulgham Bruce, Debra. "Grief and Depression." August 28, 2022. webmd.com/depression/guide/depression-grief

Acknowledgments

This book is dedicated to Mr. Reese Peanut Butter Cup–aka My Research/Writing Partner.

12/01/2012 – 08/24/2024

He was a good boy. (Really, he was-ish.)

Let's put "good" into context. He had moxie. Spitfire comes to mind—and that is why we loved him.

He enjoyed yelling at anyone walking past the house—even without seeing them, he somehow knew they were outside (I believe he had super dog powers). He despised brooms, mops, and anything with wheels. He loved clover and gardening with Mom—especially the peas and green beans, eating them as she picked. Favorite hang out space was under the trees next to the hosta. He liked Dad's socks, but more importantly stealing them from him. Piece of paper on the floor? He would kill you for it. He was a great protector, especially of Mom, anyone who was sick, and the grandchildren—he was on duty. He loved Christmas and expected the same number of presents as everyone else in the room. He took on Rottweilers although he was eight pounds, and Mom would say "Are you trying to kill us on our walk?" He talked with his eyes (usually with a deep dark stare) and would add head tilts to lighten the mood. He had girlfriends in the neighborhood (Tess and Coco). He loved Woofie his playmate and buddy—aka Pedro. He was a fan of killing his stuffed animals. He was a terror of terriers. He was well educated—loved writing with Mom, listening to her recite her book and studies over and over and over again and attending Zoom classes with her—twelve years of higher education. He deserves a masters diploma.

His time with us was not enough.

Resse-man, thank you for helping me write this book. Without your astute listening skills, glares, stares, and super many kisses, I am not sure I could have completed.

Your spirit is missed—deeply.

About J. Byrd

I am a mother, wife to the love of my life, a Mimi to the littles, professor of many, and friend of some. I enjoy gardening, decorating, kayaking, yoga, traveling, and the color green. And, according to my granddaughter, I am the Queen of Crows.

I believe nothing is static. So, embrace change. She carries you throughout life. Get used to her. It's not always pretty (sometimes it sucks), but it is. We clutch onto security and things and people for some sort of constant. Then die. For what? Touch the earth. Smell the clover. Hear the laughter of a child discovering something new. My life's work has been that of a teacher/professor. Helping others to discover their world and their voice.

It started when I was in kindergarten, coming home and repeating my lessons for the day to my stuffed animals and dolls, writing on my chalkboard in the basement. This year, as I finish writing this book, it will have been thirty-nine years serving in education—from mommy and me lessons, preschool, corporate, government, to university.

I have published and presented my academic work in the past. I have served also as a blind reviewer and copy editor for academic journals. This book is my first publication in creative writing. I sincerely hope that my work—voice—reaches you and is helpful in your personal life's journey.

Best to you,

j.

www.ingramcontent.com/pod-product-compliance
Lightning Source LLC
Chambersburg PA
CBHW021151130626
46554CB00005B/1764